...AK

Flatiron

McGonagall
Pass
△I

III △

△II

GLACIER

Mt.
...atum

Lower Icefall

THE
HALL
OF THE
MOUNTAIN KING

Mount McKinley from Wonder Lake

"Think naught of the outside world—
    From now on it's out of bounds, forbidden—
    Shun the day, its sunlight and life's giddy whirl."

—The edict of the Mountain King,
    from Ibsen's *Peer Gynt*.

THE
HALL
OF THE
MOUNTAIN KING

Howard H. Snyder

CHARLES SCRIBNER'S SONS
NEW YORK

3 5 7 9 11 13 15 17 19   c/c   20 18 16 14 12 10 8 6 4 2

Printed in the United States of America
Library of Congress Catalog Card Number 72–11145
SBN 684–13270–2 (cloth)

If you can meet with Triumph and Disaster
    And treat those two imposters just the same;
Yours is the Earth and everything that's in it,
    And—which is more—you'll be a Man, my son!

                          Rudyard Kipling

PREFACE

An expedition to a high and isolated mountain is an instance of direct human conflict with the elemental forces of the Earth, with the protective and obscuring veneer of technological civilization stripped away. This is a story of exploration into a realm where man is only a temporary and uninvited intruder, an account of a journey to the limit of man's ability to survive—and beyond.

Why do men climb mountains, taking such fearsome and sometimes tragic risks? There are probably as many answers as there are climbers. To share a climber's viewpoint one must stand in his spiked boots, and come to know the awesome beauty and the overwhelming violence of the high mountain realm. Tied vicariously into a climbing rope the reader can be taken along on a mountaineering expedition, to feel the glacier's icy breath flowing from a deep crevasse, to hear the roar of an avalanche, to kick a line of steps along the spine of a snow-covered ridge.

The author wishes to thank those who have in various ways helped and advised him. Some have read and commented on the manuscript, and others have provided information on specific points. Among them are George Perkins, Gordon Haber, John Ireton, Paul Schlichter, Jerry Lewis, Joe Wilcox, and the late Vin Hoeman. The author is indebted to Louisa Lewis and Michèle Snyder for their work in proofreading the manuscript. Special thanks are due to Dr. Horace F. Quick of the University of Colorado for first encouraging the writing of the manuscript, to Dr. David Smith of McGill University for his extensive critical suggestions, and to Dr. Bradford Washburn of Boston's Museum of Science for his help and advice both before and after the expedition.

CONTENTS

THE
HALL
OF THE
MOUNTAIN KING

INTRODUCTION

One peak dominates the Alaska Range, making 12,000-, 13,000-, and 14,000-foot peaks appear as mere hills by comparison. To some Alaskan Indians the ice-clad giant was Denali—"The Home of the Sun." We call that peak Mount McKinley, but in other times and in other tongues it was called "The Great One." Mount Foraker was called The Great One's wife, and at 17,400 feet it is McKinley's nearest rival. But even Foraker's soaring height is viewed out of proportion next to McKinley, which reaches 20,320 feet into the bitter sub-arctic air.

Mount McKinley justifies the use of superlatives, because it is the culmination point of North America; its base-to-summit elevation is the greatest of any mountain on earth; and it is one of the world's most massive peaks. The Great One does not attain its height by straining upward as a sky-piercing spire, but rather rises from a huge base and builds gradually upward like a round-shouldered pyramid. McKinley's bulk is so great that a level area which is at 19,500 feet on the north face would easily swallow up more than thirty football fields. At a latitude of 63° North, Mount McKinley is the world's highest peak above 50° latitude, and its weather and climate are therefore as severe as those found on much higher peaks in the lower latitudes of Asia.

The first ascent of Mount McKinley was made in 1910 by the famed Sourdough Expedition, which missed mountaineering immortality by choosing to climb North Peak, which is 850 feet lower than South Peak. The first ascent of South Peak was accomplished in 1913 by Archdeacon Hudson Stuck's expedition. Between that time and the late 1960's, fewer than 250 people had climbed to the summit of one or the other of McKinley's two peaks. Considering the hazards and difficulties that guard Mount McKinley's summit, the fatality count during sixty years of climbs and attempts was a surprisingly low four men. All four were killed by falls, three of which were falls into crevasses, and all of which occurred below 13,000 feet. McKinley's foremost danger, the horrendous weather on its upper slopes, had not claimed a single victim, thanks to good luck and to the exercise of caution by expeditions on the peak. But luck cannot last forever.

Many things were to change in the summer of 1967, when the Joseph F. Wilcox Mount McKinley Expedition challenged the mountain. The group witnessed nights when the hushed earth glowed under the fire of a midnight dawn, and days when death rode the wind. This is the story of that expedition, and of its tragic climb into history.

PREPARATION
Advice and Consent

It is the nature of enthusiastic mountaineers, after they have completed one successful and long-awaited climb, to start planning immediately for the next. This is a method of mental stimulation which costs nothing as long as it never advances from the thinking stage to the preparing stage. Such was my state of mind in the late summer of 1965, upon returning from a camping and climbing trip with Paul Schlichter to Yellowstone Park and the Tetons of Wyoming. When I was twelve years old, my reading of mountaineering literature had inspired several daydreams. I hoped to fulfill these dreams at some time in the unforeseeable future. After seven years of waiting, my first goal was attained when I reached the summit of Switzerland's Matterhorn. Upon returning from the Tetons, my next major goal went from the dreaming to the thinking stage. Jerry Lewis, a fellow climber and resident of Boulder, Colorado, was visiting in my home one day when he casually mentioned that he would like to go on an extended

3

trip and climb a big peak. I said, "How about McKinley, in Alaska?" Lewis replied, "I'd like that." Our goal, the summit of North America's highest peak, advanced a notch to the planning stage. The Colorado Mount McKinley Expedition was an idea, but not yet a reality.

Two endeavors were approached simultaneously as the first order of business, namely the gathering of information about Mount McKinley, and recruiting members for the expedition. The minimum expedition size allowed by the National Park Service was four men, and this minimum was met rather easily. In addition to Lewis and myself, we recruited Paul Schlichter and Steve Lewis. Schlichter was an Air Force Academy cadet, and Steve was Jerry Lewis's younger brother. Two other members of our group were forced to withdraw from the expedition. Joe Fullop, a strong and experienced climber with mountains higher than McKinley to his credit, was severely injured in a roped fall on Colorado's Maroon Bells Peaks, a fall which killed the other two men on his rope. John Ohrenschall was forced to withdraw due to the illness of his wife. Obtaining additional members was difficult, since the climbers we contacted lacked the time, money, or inclination to make the trip. Climbers with sufficient time lacked money, and those with money had jobs which they could not leave for a long enough time to go on the expedition. Several other men contacted us about going on the climb, but were considered deficient in experience and were therefore politely turned down. Thus we continued as a minimum-number, four-man expedition.

The four men of the Colorado Mount McKinley Expedition had similar experience backgrounds, since all were from Colorado. Jerry Lewis was a thirty-year-old Army veteran, studying for a degree in electrical engineering. He had traveled the world over, from the frozen desert of Greenland, to the blazing desert of Libya, to the jungles of New Guinea. Jerry had climbed many 14,000-foot peaks in Colorado, and had done some climbing in Greenland. At 6'5" tall, and weighing 220 pounds, Jerry looked like a red-headed Matt Dillon.

Steve Lewis, twenty-one, had climbed more than a dozen of Colorado's "fourteeners," including winter ascents. He had made snow-and-ice climbs with me for specific McKinley training. Steve was a student at the University of Colorado, as were Jerry Lewis and myself. Steve and I each weighed 175 pounds, and at 6'2" tall, we were the "little men" of the group.

Paul Schlichter was a First Class cadet at the U.S. Air Force Academy, ready to receive his commission as a Second Lieutenant in June of 1967. Schlichter and I were both twenty-two years old. He was a crew-cut blond, with 200 lean, strong pounds on his 6'4" frame. I had introduced Paul to climbing, and had taken him on his first climb of 14,255-foot Longs Peak. We had climbed together for five years, in Colorado, Wyoming, and Mexico. Paul counted two peaks of 17,000 feet and one of 18,000 feet among his climbs, as well as a dozen winter and summer ascents of Colorado "fourteeners."

I was the leader and fourth member of the Colorado Expedition. My college studies in geography and geology heightened my interest in and awareness of the basic ingredient of mountaineering—the mountains. I had climbed extensively in Colorado, including twenty-four ascents of Longs Peak, with at least one climb of Longs during each month of the year. In the Alps I had climbed eleven peaks, among them the Matterhorn, Monte Rosa, the Eiger, and Mont Blanc. In addition to thirty-eight ascents of "fourteeners," my experience included climbs of two 15,000-foot peaks, two 17,000-foot peaks, and one of 18,000 feet.

I gathered all of the information I could about Mount McKinley, by reading the accounts of Belmore Browne's and Hudson Stuck's early efforts on the peak as well as Bradford Washburn's more recent climbs; by talking with local men who had climbed McKinley; and by scrutinizing many maps of the peak. Any questions raised or left unanswered by this research were asked in a long series of letters to Arthur J. Hayes, Chief Park Ranger at Mount McKinley National Park.

Planning and preparation for climbing Mount McKinley occupied the major share of my time for two years. Equipment lists were made out, menus were written, transportation costs were figured. Every step was modified, checked, and re-checked dozens of times. Correspondence and equipment plans filled three legal-size tablets, and equipment purchases were made from over a dozen suppliers. We were determined to leave as little as possible to chance, to spend our time and money in such a manner as to give us the best opportunity for safety and success.

We made preliminary orders of food, camping equipment, climbing gear, and clothing. On the basis of tests we made some changes in our final orders, including discarding butane stoves in favor of kerosene stoves, and deleting some foodstuffs found unpalatable by one or more of our group. While testing army Korean boots in December of 1965, I was caught by darkness on 14,255-foot Longs Peak, in Rocky Mountain National Park. My younger brother Bob and I spent the night at 13,700 feet, and I sustained frostbite on four toes. The Korean boots were eliminated from our equipment list.

Our final equipment list included such items as army felt boots, down parkas and pants, emergency flares and mirrors, a pressure cooker, plastic snowshoes, and a tent which had been used by the successful Winter McKinley Expedition the previous February. We made a direct order to Germany for special adjustable crampons, designed to fit both our low-altitude rubber boots and our high-altitude felt boots.

Our training for McKinley included conditioning ourselves so that we would be capable of strenuous activity at high elevations for extended periods. Paul Schlichter and I made a climbing trip to Mexico in December of 1966, in order to get into physical condition, and to familiarize ourselves with the rigors of high altitudes. We climbed Orizaba (18,619 feet), Popocatepetl (17,887 feet), and Ixtaccihuatl (17,343 feet), which are the third, fifth, and seventh highest mountains in North America.

Our preparations had been extensive and meticulous. I had climbed with all of the men of our group many times, including winter ascents of 14,000-foot peaks. I knew the men well, and I was willing to stake my life on their actions and judgment. Whether he is willing to or not, a man literally puts his life on the line when he ties into a climbing rope with his companions. Every man in our group had a well-developed sense of humor, a valuable asset on an isolated and hazardous climb. The men and the equipment were hand-picked, and I had confidence in the performance of both. We were ready, and if the weather favored us on Mount McKinley, we felt that we were capable of launching a successful assault on the peak.

The Alaska Rescue Group (ARG), whom we had requested to serve as the support party for our expedition, informed us that they were concerned by the small size of our party. They suggested that we check into the possibility of combining with the Joseph F. Wilcox Mount McKinley Expedition, which was a nine-man expedition that was climbing McKinley via the same route we were, and at the same time.

On 20 April 1967, I received a letter from Joseph F. Wilcox, the twenty-four-year-old leader of the expedition that bore his name. Wilcox suggested that our two groups share expenses on radios and fixed ropes. I was agreeable to such an arrangement, and replied to that effect. I said that sharing radios, however, would require a definite coordination of our expeditions, so that we would have continual access to the radios. Wilcox also suggested the possibility of our becoming a part of his group. He said he could make no commitments about a combination without first reviewing our experience forms, which were the Park Service climbing application forms. He enclosed the autobiographies of his group, along with the mimeographed letters and plans ("M-forms") which he regularly sent out to the members of his expedition.

We were interested in coordination, not combination, and I made this clear in letters to Wilcox, the ARG, and the Park Service. I sent copies of our group's experience forms to Wilcox, and asked that he send me copies of his group's forms. Wilcox returned our forms as requested, but he did not send copies of theirs.

I was a bit unsure about the Wilcox group, due to several things in their letters and M-forms. The proposed menus of the Wilcox Expedition caused some wonder when it was noted that chili was scheduled for consumption high on the mountain. The group's food was high in starch, and appeared none too tasty.

The most disturbing revelation was that the Wilcox group was planning to establish camps on both summits simultaneously. I could think of no worse place to camp than on the cold, windswept summits of

North America's highest peak. It was also hard to imagine a more disaster-prone arrangement than that of having a split party perched on the widely separated summits of Mount McKinley.

In his letters, and later in telephone conversations, Wilcox stressed that our group would be faster than his. How could he possibly have known how fast we might be? He did not know us personally, nor did he know how much equipment we would be carrying. I could only assume that he expected his group to be quite slow.

Wilcox also seemed to feel that his proposed climb had unique publicity value, and was expecting news media coverage of the expedition. An ascent of Mount McKinley is a tremendous personal accomplishment, and it has been done by very few people. However, it had been done often enough that it no longer warranted headlines. When I told friends that I was going to climb Mount McKinley, they often said, "I suppose we'll be reading about it in the papers." I replied, "I hope not, because if you do, it means something has gone wrong."

Wilcox wrote to Bradford Washburn, the world's foremost Mount McKinley authority, asking if some of his expedition's proposed activities had been done previously:

> I will be leading a nine man expedition on Mount McKinley this June. It appears that we will receive considerable publicity from area newspapers and TV stations to the extent that they may send men to Alaska to cover the expedition. They seem excited by the fact that we may put a camp on the summit, climb both summits simultaneously, or put a camp on each summit. According to the Park Service, some climbers spent the night on the summit in 1960.
>
> To the best of you [sic] knowledge
>   1.   has anyone else spent the night on the summit?
>   2.   has any group climbed both peaks simultaneously?
>   3.   has anyone camped on the north summit?
>   4.   has anyone camped on both summits simultaneously?

Your help will be greatly appreciated. I do not want my group to claim a "first" unless it is, indeed, a "first." Please reply soon, because the news media are anxious to start releases.

Not surprisingly, Washburn got the impression that the Wilcox Expedition's sole purpose was to gain publicity. Washburn replied in part: "A Japanese party spent a very comfortable night on top of the South Peak and another party climbed both peaks of McKinley in the same day. In fact, the 1942 Army Expedition and our 1947 expedition lived comfortably for literally weeks above 15,000 feet, and could easily have spent a week or more on top of either or both peaks if we had had the slightest inclination to do so—or any conceivable practical reason for it. After all, climbers have spent week after week on Everest, K-2, Nanga Parabat and scores of other Himalayan giants far in excess of McKinley's altitude, packing heavy loads and climbing difficult rock and ice simply for the sheer love of it—not just sleeping their way into headlines!" Washburn closed with the observation that McKinley had never been climbed blindfolded or backwards, nor had any party of nine ever fallen simultaneously into the same crevasse.

This unfortunate misunderstanding between a veteran mountaineer and an unfledged expedition leader was to have some far-reaching and long-lasting side effects.

Due to the relatively limited high-altitude ice-climbing experience of some of the members of the Wilcox Expedition, the Park Service made its approval of the climb subject to certain conditions. The conditions were that the expedition carry a radio and extra batteries; that the party not be split into two groups, with the most experienced people in one group and the least experienced in the other, as had been planned; and that the less experienced members receive several days of intensive training on Mount Rainier.

The doubtful plans of the Wilcox Expedition, when considered carefully and individually, did not necessarily constitute a major hazard. However, taken together they were enough to make me glad that the Colorado Expedition would have separate food, equipment, and personnel, and that we would be coordinated with the Wilcox group rather than combined. Coordination left us free to exercise our own judgment during the climb; it left us as a distinct and viable entity, free to join with the Wilcox group in such activities as were deemed mutually beneficial.

One night in the first week of June, our best laid plans went awry. Jerry Lewis and I were at his house, packing man-day food packages.[1] We worked far past midnight, and I wondered where Steve Lewis might be at such an hour, as he had not yet returned home. At about 22:00 [2] that evening, Steve had been involved in an automobile accident. He had received a broken hand in the wreck, and our expedition's independence snapped along with the bone in Steve's hand. We had fallen below the minimum four-man expedition requirement set by the National Park Service. After two years of painstaking and expensive planning and preparation, our expedition was ground to a halt within twelve hours of our intended departure for Alaska.

I talked the situation over with Jerry Lewis and Paul Schlichter. We were no longer numerically qualified as an independent expedition. Our alternatives were to go climbing as a three-man group in the interior ranges of British Columbia (a possibility which I had investigated on the remote chance that just such a circumstance should arise), or to combine with the Wilcox group. The dilemma required an immediate answer; we had to either combine with the Wilcox Expedition, or we had to abandon the hopes, plans, and expenditures of the past two years. We had some vague and minor apprehensions about the Wilcox group, but they were overpowered by our desire not to turn our backs on two years of work, so we decided to telephone Wilcox and explain our situation to him. After all, via the Muldrow Glacier route, Mount McKinley is not a technically difficult peak, and with proper exercise of caution and common sense, what could possibly endanger such a large and well-equipped group? Weeks later, this question was answered, to our horror.

I telephoned Wilcox in Puyallup, Washington, and told him of our situation. He had seen our experience forms, and was therefore agreeable to a combination. We both sent letters to the National Park Service

[1] A man-day food package contained all of the food necessary for the Colorado Expedition for one day. They weighed eight pounds each.

[2] All times in this book are on the basis of the twenty-four-hour clock, since they are kept that way in the climbing log books to avoid confusion. In Alaska, with twenty to twenty-four hours of daylight in the summer, AM and PM quickly lose significance.

regarding our combination. The Colorado group was to maintain separate food and equipment, but it was no longer an expedition that could act alone. We were members of the Joseph F. Wilcox Mount McKinley Expedition, for better or worse.

APPROACH
Roads, Rivers, and Tundra

Jerry Lewis and I proceeded to make the modifications in our food and equipment which were necessitated by our reduction to a three-man group. We packed Lewis's new Dodge Power Wagon with all of our gear, and left Boulder on 9 June. Steve Lewis's withdrawal from the expedition had left room for Schlichter in the truck, but he had previously arranged to travel as far as Pasco, Washington, with his Academy roommate. We already had all of Schlichter's equipment packed in the truck when we left Boulder, and we picked him up in Pasco on the tenth. We were carrying a boxful of plastic Snowtread snowshoes, which are made in Boulder. Ten and a half pairs of the snowshoes were Wilcox's, and they were delivered in time due only to the lucky circumstance that our group was going from Boulder to Mount McKinley. When we met Schlichter in Pasco, I told him that we had thirteen and one-half pairs of snowshoes in the truck. He replied, "Thirteen and a half pairs. An amputee in the group."

12

We reached Mount Rainier National Park, our rendezvous point with the Wilcox group, on the morning of 11 June. The entire park was shrouded in heavy fog which sometimes made it impossible to see the road more than ten feet ahead. We drove to Park Headquarters at Longmire, and sought information as to the Wilcox party's whereabouts. The rangers told us that Wilcox was engaged in snow-technique practice on the mountain. I asked if there were any letters for me at the Longmire Inn, since I was expecting a reply from Berle Mercer regarding the packing in of our equipment in McKinley Park. There was no letter. I later found out that Wilcox had claimed the letter, opened and read it, and then stored it with his files. I was finally able to read the letter a week later, when Wilcox gave it to me upon arrival at Wonder Lake at the foot of Mount McKinley.

The fog cleared in the afternoon, and Mount Rainier stood out boldly against a bright blue sky, tier upon tier of shattered ice thrusting up into the clear air. We were to view numerous scenes of this kind as the summer wore on. That afternoon, at Cougar Rock Campground, we had our first meeting with Joe Wilcox. He drove up to our campsite, and I walked to his car to greet him. I said a cheery hello, and introduced myself. Wilcox said nothing. He sat in his car, unsmiling, and surveyed me like a Hong Kong tailor sizing up a customer. With Wilcox were Mark McLaughlin, Dennis Luchterhand, and Anshel Schiff. McLaughlin, a friendly and outgoing sort of fellow, broke the awkward silence by bounding out of the car and introducing himself to us. Schiff, Luchterhand, and Wilcox followed suit rather mechanically.

Wilcox asked where we were spending the night, and I replied that we thought we would stay in Rainier Park, and then meet him at his in-laws' house in Puyallup, Washington, the next morning. Wilcox preferred that we proceed immediately to Puyallup and spend the night there. We agreed, and the Wilcox group departed. We hardly knew what to think about our first meeting. Only one of their group had been friendly, and Wilcox had been nothing less than brusque in his manner. No one had proffered so much as a "thank you" for the "special delivery" snowshoes we had brought them. Lewis said, "If they're going to be ornery we just won't go." Schlichter suggested, not wholly in jest, "We should call home and have Steve put on the first jet for Seattle." We broke camp and drove on to Puyallup.

In Puyallup we met the rest of the Wilcox Expedition. Despite the time it took for us to break camp, we had arrived before Wilcox, so we had an informal meeting and discussion with the men who were present. After nearly an hour, Wilcox arrived with the rest of the group.

F. Jerry Clark, thirty-one, was the oldest and most experienced member of the Wilcox group. Clark had climbed extensively in the Wyoming Rockies, and had done a little climbing in Colorado. He had gained good ice-climbing experience in the Cascades of Washington and Oregon, and had managed to squeeze in a climb while on a non-mountaineering expedition to Antarctica. He was an Indiana native and a graduate of Purdue University, and was now living in Eugene, Oregon. Clark had been designated as the deputy leader of the expedition. His thoughtful and well-informed letters to me before the trip had impressed me, and he was no less impressive in person. He had an intelligent and active mind, and a very friendly manner. Clark was small, 5'7" tall and 145 pounds in weight, but small size is no drawback on a mountain climb. Unfortunately, his physical conditioning had been inadequate, and he was physically unequal to the demands of a very strenuous climb such as Mount McKinley. This inequality was soon in evidence on the mountain.

Henry "Hank" Janes, twenty-five, and Mark McLaughlin, twenty-three, were close friends of Clark, and had climbed and camped with him numerous times. They both displayed Clark's tendency to move slowly on the trail, but whether this was coincidence or training is open to question. McLaughlin (6'½", 150 pounds) was the friendliest man in the Wilcox group, with a ready smile and a sincere laugh. He was one of the more experienced men, having made many ascents in the Cascades, and by almost any standard an excellent expedition man. McLaughlin was a long-time resident of Eugene, Oregon.

Janes was small (5'5", 140 pounds), and his manner was quiet and reserved. He was by no means unfriendly, but he did not force his presence or his observations on anyone, waiting rather for an invitation to "join in." Janes was an Indiana native and a Purdue graduate, and was now teaching in the public school system of Portland, Oregon. His experience was varied and adequate, including ascents in the Colorado and Wyoming Rockies and in the Cascades.

Dennis Luchterhand, twenty-four, was tall (6'4") and lean (175 pounds), one of the fastest and strongest men in the Wilcox group. His experience was minimal, as was that of John Russell, twenty-three. Luchterhand's experience consisted of two summer climbing trips in the Wyoming Rockies, and summer climbs of five small Austrian peaks. He had done no climbing for more than a year before the Wilcox group's shakedown climbs on Mount Rainier. Luchterhand was a graduate of the University of Wisconsin. He had ranged far and wide during his early days, and Scarsdale, New York was his current home-base.

Russell had made a half-dozen climbs in the Cascades. He lived in Eugene, Oregon, and had contacted Clark when he heard about the planned expedition. Russell was very loud and uninhibited in his comments. He had a full-to-overflowing head of curly reddish-blond hair, and a beard to match. He lacked only an eye patch to complete the image of a buccaneer. Russell weighed 165 pounds and stood 5'9" tall.

Walter Taylor, twenty-four, and Stephen Taylor, twenty-two, were as different as two men could be, and were rather obviously not related. Both men weighed 155 pounds, but Walt Taylor's weight was concentrated in his 5'8" height, whereas Steve Taylor's was spread thinly over his 6'2" height. Walt Taylor was a quick-witted man with a wry sense of humor. Although his experience was only fair, he proved to be the best acclimatized, fastest climber in the Wilcox group, and an excellent expedition man. Walt Taylor was another Indianan, a Purdue graduate, and a long-time friend of Jerry Clark. He had done summer climbs in the Wyoming and Colorado Rockies for several years.

Steve Taylor had met Wilcox in a class at Brigham Young University in Provo, Utah, where both were students. Wilcox had interested him in climbing, and in the proposed McKinley expedition. Taylor had graduated from BYU just a few weeks before the expedition started for Alaska. He was the junior member of the expedition, in both age and experience, and his mannerisms bespoke a man very unsure of himself. His experience before the Rainier shakedown consisted of one climb of

11,750-foot Mount Timpanogos, in Utah. The Park Service balked at S. Taylor's qualifications, but Wilcox wrote a letter stating that Taylor was actually far more experienced than his climbing application indicated. The Park Service relented, and Taylor was permitted to go on the climb.

Anshel Schiff, thirty, was another member of the Wilcox group whose experience was so slight that one wonders why he was allowed to go on the climb. One possible reason is that Schiff (as well as Steve Taylor) was originally in the "scientific" branch of the expedition, and was to have gone no higher than 11,000 feet on the Muldrow Glacier. Schiff's experience consisted of three climbs in Wyoming, the most significant of which was an ascent of the Grand Teton as the client of a professional guide. Schiff carried 175 poorly conditioned pounds on his 5'10" frame. He was slow, and could carry only half to three-quarter loads. Schiff did, however, exhibit good judgment concerning his own capabilities. He was the only man in the Wilcox group to speak out frequently and strongly about the misuse of equipment on the climb. Schiff was another Purdue graduate, and was an assistant professor at the university.

Joseph Wilcox, twenty-four, was the leader of the expedition, a sturdy 6'1" tall and weighing 180 pounds. He was a Kansas native, and was now a resident of Provo, Utah. He was the only married man in the expedition. Wilcox had ascended five different peaks in Washington and Oregon, including six ascents of Mount Rainier. He had made two winter ascents in Utah and Nevada. He possessed a strange idea of the publicity value of his climbing exploits, particularly his proposed climb of Mount McKinley. Wilcox was less experienced than a number of the men in his group, and was the leader of the expedition because he was the organizer and primary planner. He provided a sharp personality contrast with the expedition's deputy leader, the gregarious Jerry Clark.

On the trail, Wilcox proved to be a strong and steady climber, but he became progressively slower with increasing altitude above 12,000 feet. None of the men in the Wilcox group had climbed higher than 14,410 feet (Mount Rainier), and above 12,000 feet on Mount McKin-

ley the altitude took a heavy toll on the energies of all of them except
Walt Taylor.

Shortly after Wilcox arrived in Puyallup, we got down to discussing
the details of our combination. I did not know at the time what experience the Wilcox party members had, since Wilcox had not sent me
their experience forms as I had requested.

Steve Taylor was against our combination, and by interjecting various comments he seemed to be trying to use the occasion to gain ac-
ceptance into the group, as a mountaineer among mountaineers. I
know now that he was worried not only by the combination, but about
the whole trip, since the entire endeavor was completely foreign to
him. He brought up a number of inane situations regarding the inter-
mixing of personnel and equipment, and wanted to know what we
would do in each case. I was taken aback by Taylor's apparent lack of
basic mountaineering knowledge. Days later, I came to realize that he
was speaking from a wealth of inexperience.

W. Taylor was uneasy about the combination at first, but became
convinced of our good intentions as the discussion wore on. The main
concern seemed to be that we would trip gaily up the trail with our
group's lighter gear, and leave the Wilcox group laboring under their
Herculean loads. We assured them that we would be perfectly happy
to help carry their equipment, and this eliminated what they considered to be a major problem. Wilcox had elaborate plans for switching
tent mates at every camp, and wanted my agreement on the total in-
terchangeability of food and equipment. I agreed subject to the stipu-
lation that Colorado group food and equipment would be used by Colorado group personnel whenever possible.

McLaughlin was very much in favor of the combination, and repeated several times that their's was a "mail-order expedition," mean-
ing that previously unacquainted people had been brought together by
mail for the expedition. Clark was calm, and his comments were well
reasoned.

Wilcox went over the Colorado group equipment and food list with
me. He asked how much food we were taking, and I told him that we
had enough for thirty days above McGonagall Pass, where the Mul-

drow Glacier is first encountered. Our menus consisted of low-weight, high-calorie items, and could easily be stretched if a storm forced us to remain in a camp. Our food weighed 3½ pounds per man-day, including one bag of bulk items that were not man-day packaged. Wilcox stated that his group had enough food to stay on the mountain for sixty days. Such a prospect not only surprised me, it frightened me. "Why would you want to spend sixty days on Mount McKinley?" I asked. Wilcox replied, "Some parties have had to spend as much as seventeen days waiting out a storm at 18,000 feet. Our planning has allowed for that. We want twenty days of food above 15,000 feet."

I had never heard of a party spending that much time in a storm high on McKinley. This plan disturbed me for several days, until I found out that it was an overly ambitious statement, partly intended to induce us to accede to Wilcox's total assimilation of our equipment. The Wilcox party was using its prepackaged food for several days before we reached McGonagall Pass, and by the time the Colorado group started using its food supplies it had thirty days of food to the Wilcox group's thirty-one.

Wilcox and I adjourned from the backyard to the kitchen, and worked out a written agreement. The rest of the Wilcox group set to work packing their food and equipment in their trailer, and the backyard hummed with the activity of a combat staging area. The Colorado group paid $92.00 as our share of the expedition radio and fixed rope expenses, then departed for a campground on Puget Sound. We arrived at the campground at 03:00, and settled down for a short but sound night's sleep.

On 12 June, we drove on to Seattle and did some last-minute shopping for extra goggles, plastic fuel cans, and mosquito repellent. We then continued on northward into Canada, through the Cariboo region of British Columbia, then eastward across the mountains to Dawson Creek and Milepost Zero of the Alaska Highway.

On 14 June, we started north on the Alaska Highway, 1,300 miles of dusty but excellent gravel road. Our truck's color varied from white, to tan, to gray, to black, depending on the color of the earth on a given stretch of the road. The next day we spotted the Wilcox party's old Chevrolet carryall and Hank Janes's Dodge camper-van parked beside the road at Teslin Lake, Yukon Territory. They had stopped to replace a flat tire on the trailer. We talked with them for a while, and found out that they had left Seattle twenty-four hours after we did. They had been driving twenty-four hours a day, which was as Wilcox had planned it.

We stopped for the night at Wolf Creek Campground just outside Whitehorse. We saw Wilcox's Chevrolet blitz by with the trailer jouncing along behind. Later, at a much more sedate pace, Janes's van came by, and pulled into our campsite. Clark, Janes, and McLaughlin visited for a spell, and Clark said there was dissension in the ranks over Wilcox's non-stop driving. They drove on, and we settled down for a leisurely meal and a good night's sleep.

On the morning of 16 June, we continued on up the Alcan to White-horse, where we bought the last of our expedition supplies. We purchased canned butter, slab bacon, candy bars, and kerosene and alcohol for the stoves. As an indication of Yukon price scales, it is interesting to note that kerosene cost U.S. $1.00 per U.S. gallon.

The last forty miles of the Canadian section of the Alcan was the only poor part of the road, being strewn with washboard molehills which were striving for mountain status. We reached the Yukon-Alaska border at 19:21, and the smooth pavement of Alaska was a welcome change. We zoomed along into the unending daylight of the Alaskan summer, and were making excellent time. At Northway, about fifty miles inside Alaska, we were flagged down by a frantic Wilcox party.

The old Chevrolet, which we had nicknamed the "Green Bomb," had broken under the strain of fast, non-stop driving. Wilcox wanted us to tow their trailer to Wonder Lake in Mount McKinley National Park, a distance of about 500 miles, including 254 miles of gravel road. We agreed to tow the trailer, and the Wilcox party paid to have a bumper fabricated from scrap steel and bolted onto Lewis's truck. I mentioned to Wilcox that this would cut down on our gas mileage, and he offered to exchange some of his group's food for the tow, thus balancing the food supplies of our two groups. In fact, we did not need the food trade, but we felt that this agreement would cement our combination, and aid us in getting acquainted with the men of the Wilcox group. While the bumper was being attached, the Wilcox group fell to packing their gear into the trailer.

We camped that night at Moon Lake Campground, west of Tok, Alaska. I took a picture of our tent and the lake at 23:35, by the light of the midnight sun.

On the morning of the seventeenth, we continued along the Alcan to its intersection with the Richardson Highway at Delta Junction. To the south, the ice-robed giants of the eastern Alaska Range shimmered in the bright sunshine. We were in real mountain country at last. As we drove southward on the Richardson Highway, the beautiful and forbiddingly steep peaks of the central Alaska Range became visible.

Wilcox had been delayed, trying to find a place to buy white gasoline for his group's expedition stoves. He had even talked of calling Fairbanks and having the gas sent to McKinley Park on the Alaska Railroad. When we reached Paxson, at the start of the Denali Highway, we noticed that the service station there had cans of white gas stacked along two walls.

The trailer was a real hazard on the Denali Highway, which was a hilly, gravel road. It was much too heavily loaded, and the hitch was too high, causing further unbalance. On downhill stretches, the trailer would start to weave behind the truck, and would finally gain enough momentum to start the truck weaving a half cycle out of phase, to the left when the trailer swerved right and vice versa. Applying the brakes only made the oscillation worse.

We got our first view of Mount McKinley from about 140 miles west of Paxson. We were still well over 100 airline miles from the peak. After many years of reading about Mount McKinley, it was a real thrill to gaze at its massive form, crouched on the horizon in the afternoon haze. In spite of the distance and the haze, I could identify North and South Peaks, Karstens Ridge, the three icefalls of the Harper Glacier, Denali Pass, and Archdeacons Tower.

By mid-afternoon we reached McKinley Park and the National Park Headquarters. We stopped at the Park Information Center, where we learned that a Japanese party had climbed McKinley in five days via the West Buttress, and a Minnesota group had done the South Wall in twelve days. Both expeditions had been flown in to the base of the mountain. The weather had been phenomenal—two weeks of calm, clear conditions. The mild, clear weather had caused a great deal of melting, and the McKinley River was reported to be very high. We had to cross the river to get to the mountain, so we were concerned about the news. The content of Wilcox's letter to Washburn, asking what "firsts" his party might accomplish was common knowledge among the Park rangers. The ranger at the Information Center told us that Wilcox made himself out to be "God's gift to Mount McKinley" in the letter.

We made a brief stop to confer with Chief Park Ranger Arthur J. Hayes, and to thank him for his help to our group over the course of two years of preparation. Mr. Hayes said that he would be flying over us once in a while during our climb.

The drive to Wonder Lake, 84 miles from the village of McKinley Park, was beautiful and exciting. We saw moose, caribou, Dall sheep, and a lone porcupine. Approaching as we were from the northeast, we were able to look up the length of the Muldrow and Harper Glaciers, our proposed route to the top. The peak loomed ever larger on the horizon, a breathtaking monument to nature, sculpted in ice. As we neared the stagnant, grass-covered snout of the Muldrow Glacier where it approaches the road, we witnessed one of the vanishing dramas of this earth, a large-scale migration of a herd of wild animals. Hundreds of magnificent caribou ambled slowly along on the tundra, against the backdrop of the ice-clad form of the continent's highest peak.

At 22:15 we reached the Wonder Lake Ranger Station. Here we met Wayne Merry, McKinley Park's climbing ranger. In typical Alaskan manner, Merry was friendly and accommodating. He introduced us to Berle Mercer, the packer who was to transport our gear across the tundra to McGonagall Pass. Mercer was another friendly Alaskan, his sun-tanned face accented with a twinkling smile. As we talked about the climb and about packing in our gear, Merry suggested that we take pictures of Mount McKinley, which was turning pink in the pale blush of the setting sun. He knew this country well, and a beautiful sunset on a clear day is not a particularly common phenomenon around Mount McKinley.

We set up our tent at the south end of Wonder Lake, four miles from the Ranger Station. We tried to get some sleep, despite the visual stimulation of Mount McKinley at our front door, and the midnight sun at the back.

The next morning, 18 June, the Wilcox group arrived. The day was spent sorting, checking, and packing gear. Wilcox's people and equipment were to go in to the peak the next day, while the Colorado group waited at Wonder Lake until 22 June to accompany the second pack-in. Wilcox had some "scientific" work planned, measuring flow rates on the Muldrow Glacier. Since Lewis had extensive experience in surveying, Wilcox decided that Lewis should go in with the first group, to get the scientific work done at McGonagall Pass. S. Taylor was to stay with Schlichter and me, and go in with us three days later. After a briefing by Schiff on the scientific procedures and equipment, Lewis told me, "We're not going to be able to get any worthwhile information with this gear." I agreed, and confided that I had suspected as much a few weeks earlier, after reading the "research prospectus." Expert studies of the Muldrow had been made before, and I could see nothing in the prospectus that would be either new or improved. The scientific work, we soon found out, was largely an attempt to get permission for aircraft support, which is denied for all but "scientific" expeditions. Most expeditions circumvent this prohibition by flying in from the south side of the peak, and landing outside the Park boundary.

We had the first of a series of "expedition meetings" on the afternoon of the eighteenth. We sat on the ground as Wilcox talked about the objectives, decision making, and general philosophy of the expedition. He said that the group was not working as a team, but rather as individuals; that "You have seen how big the peak is, and now you're preoccupied with getting your *own* gear ready instead of working for the group." W. Taylor asked what group work there was to be done, and Wilcox could think of none. W. Taylor then made one of the most apt and significant statements of the trip: "The trouble is we don't move, we don't get busy and *do* things. No one even opens cans with gusto around here." The Colorado group had discussed this malaise on the last day's drive to the Park. I caught Schlichter's eye, and we nodded our eyelids in agreement. We were glad to see that W. Taylor was aware of the problem too, and were hopeful that he could help cure it.

Mosquitoes, the bane of the far north, made any prolonged immobility in the open a miserable task. During the meeting, I sat cross-legged to present as little surface area as possible, and wore a head net. Still, the squadrons of miniscule blood tankers managed to hit home. They coated my ankles, standing wing-to-wing, and drilled through my thick socks. After the meeting, I had charming matched anklets in the form of maddening welts.

Merry drove from his ranger station to our camp on the afternoon of the eighteenth. He brought with him a manuscript copy of Bradford Washburn's brand new *Guide to the Muldrow Route*. Merry asked Wilcox, "Would you like to see what the no-gooder has to say about the peak?" This was in reference to the legend written in the dust on the back of Janes's camper-van: "Brad is a no-gooder and a do-badder." The book was passed around, and the pictures were studied. However, since they were busy preparing for the pack-in the next morning, not one member of the Wilcox group took time to read the advice of an expert concerning the Muldrow route.

In the course of conversations with Clark and McLaughlin, I found out that Steve Taylor was the only member of the group whom Wilcox had known before the trip. All of the others were friends and acquaintances of Clark. McLaughlin explained that Wilcox had organized the expedition, but Clark had recruited almost all of the members. I asked if that didn't put Wilcox in the position of leading an expedition that was more nearly Clark's than his own. McLaughlin replied, "Yeah, that's about it."

Mercer arrived at the camp at 07:15 on 19 June, with eight pack horses. Between 1,000 and 1,050 pounds of Wilcox's gear was loaded up, and Mercer started down the trail for the McKinley River. The river was reported to be higher than the rangers had ever seen it before, so Wilcox, McLaughlin, and Russell hiked the two and a half miles to the river to check the situation out. The river was evidently well broken up into its braided channels, because they crossed without difficulty. Wilcox radioed back to the camp and requested that Schlichter, S. Taylor, and I carry the advance team's packs to the riverbank. Following the advance team's report, the nine of us who had waited at Wonder Lake squeezed ourselves and our gear into Janes's van and rode about a mile to the trail head.

Lewis, Schlichter, and I started together across the marshy meadows and through the spruce forest. We moved rapidly, to outrun the mosquitoes and to get to the river in time to take pictures of the pack string making the crossing. Lewis stopped to don his head net, but I hurried on, not wanting to stop long enough for the mosquitoes to begin prospecting. We ground off the mosquito-ridden two and a half miles to the bank of the McKinley River in about an hour. We stopped on the bank and looked across the vast riverbed. The McKinley River was divided into more than a dozen channels, writhing serpents winding their way to the sea.

We descended the low bank of the river, and started walking across the dry riverbed. The south bank was one mile distant. We were walking on the bed of a river as wide as the Mississippi. We were thankful that it was largely dry. After about a quarter mile of walking on the riverbed, we encountered the first large flowing channel of the stream. The advance team met us here. We had carried their 50- to 60-pound packs for over two miles. McLaughlin beamed a cheerful "thanks" for the effort. Back on the north bank, the rest of the men started appearing at the edge of the forest and making their way toward us over the dry riverbed. There were many demarcation lines and points on our climb, and this was the first. The McKinley River constitutes a major obstacle and hazard in the climb of Mount McKinley from the north. Crossing it is difficult and dangerous; beyond it is the realm of the mountaineer.

Schlichter, S. Taylor, and I wished the first party good traveling, and they started across the river. We watched until they had safely gained the opposite bank, about three-quarters of a mile distant, then we started back to Wonder Lake.

Schlichter and I moved along the trail at a nominal pace, stopping for drinks from cold, clear springs along the way, and to take pictures of Mount McKinley. The peak was beginning to weave a cloak of clouds around its shoulders. Even with our moderate pace, and with no packs on our backs, S. Taylor could not keep up. He kept falling behind, walking with his shoulders slumped, his head hung down, and his feet scuffing the ground. I wrote in my logbook that day that Taylor was "so slow, so morose."

He was in a continual state of depression. It was not until weeks later that I knew the reason for S. Taylor's state of mind and body. He had so very little experience that he was terrified by the sight of this icy behemoth that he was to climb, and it was literally worrying him sick. Steve Taylor was a fine young man, with strong convictions of faith, and a kind and gentle nature, but he was no match for the technical and physical challenge of Mount McKinley. With a few years of good experience he might have been a "tiger," but sending him to do battle with McKinley at this time was akin to asking a non-swimmer to tackle the English Channel.

Upon our return to Wonder Lake, Schlichter and I took advantage of the warm afternoon sun and a curious lack of mosquitoes to take sponge baths in the lake. The mosquitoes appeared in their normal multitudes later in the afternoon. The mosquitoes were so bad that we wore our head nets almost continuously, not even removing them to drink. Sleeping was difficult, because the sun went down for only one hour. Our tent was strictly a winter or high-altitude tent, and it had no mosquito netting. Therefore we were forced to keep the doors closed, and the tent became hot and musty. Outside, the mosquitoes droned on loudly and incessantly, sounding like a humming dynamo.

On 20 June, Schlichter and I took Janes's van to the Wonder Lake Ranger Station. We both read Washburn's guide, and I copied the route directions. We then walked the four miles back to camp. Our weather charm failed us that evening. Waves of rain-laden clouds swept down from McKinley, lashing the tundra with intense downpours. I looked off toward McGonagall Pass, and thought that the party there was probably catching a real soaking. Nonetheless, we would rather have been at McGonagall Pass than enduring the inactivity, heat, and mosquitoes at Wonder Lake.

The rain continued until noon the next day. I drove to Camp Denali, just beyond the Wonder Lake Ranger Station, and picked up Berle Mercer and his packing equipment. Returning to our campsite, Mercer, Schlichter, and I packed all of the Colorado group food bags, fuel, and a few other items in preparation for packing in the next morning. I went through my personal equipment, checking everything against the list I had prepared. As I was checking equipment, a rainstorm swept in with surprising speed from the direction of Mount McKinley, and I was soaked through while scurrying around to get our gear under cover.

Mercer weighed and loaded all of our gear on the morning of 22 June. The Colorado group gear that was to be packed in by horse weighed 415 pounds, whereas the Wilcox group had 1900 pounds. We drove our truck to the ranger station, and locked our extra gear in the cab. Wayne Merry drove Schlichter and me back to the trail head, and as we neared the trail we saw S. Taylor waiting for us. He was a picture of abject despondency, and Merry said, as though he was addressing Taylor: "Don't cry."

We thanked Merry for his help, said goodbye and started down the trail toward the McKinley River. McGonagall Pass and the Muldrow Glacier were eighteen miles away. I explained to Taylor that we wanted to hurry so that we could meet Mercer as he crossed the river, in case we needed a ride across the deeper channels. Schlichter and I reached the bank of the river, picked up spruce poles for balance when wading, and moved a little distance out onto the riverbed. We waited for Taylor to appear at the edge of the forest, as he had already fallen behind. We came to the edge of the first large flowing channel and noticed that it was swollen from the rains of the previous two days. We looked upstream and saw a dense curtain of rain falling at the river's headwaters, where it emerged from the Muldrow Glacier.

We took off our socks and slipped our bare feet back into our rubber boots. With our pantlegs rolled up to our hips, we stepped into the river. We crossed the river channels in a generally upstream direction, looking for the widest and most shallow points, and avoiding the downstream ends of islands due to the danger of quicksand. After crossing each channel we would stop on an island and stand on one leg like a stork, while raising the other leg behind us to drain the cold water from our boots. Streams which flow directly out of glaciers are not crystal-clear and clean, but are chocolate-brown and choked with silt and angular pebbles. These sharp rocks washed into our boots and made for very painful walking, especially since we were carrying 75-pound packs. Schlichter sustained a large gash on the sole of one of his feet as a result of the cutting effect of the gravel.

When we were about halfway across the river, we saw Mercer's pack string emerge from the forest on the north bank. Mercer's twelve-year-old son Kurt was riding with him, and a ranch guest from Camp Denali was walking alongside. S. Taylor was far behind, a small red speck that never seemed to move. We crossed two large channels, a bit touch-and-go, with an occasional flash of anxiety that the current was going to overwhelm us. To allow rapid escape in case of a fall, we did not buckle our Kelty packs' waist straps, and therefore the entire weight rested on our shoulders. We reached the last big channel of the river, within 100 yards of the south bank, and decided to wait for Mercer to arrive with the cavalry. The channel was just too deep and swift to try on foot. We yelled to Taylor not to try the last two channels we had crossed, and to wait for Mercer to bring him across.

As Mercer was crossing the last channel we had waded, the last horse on the string was knocked down by the current. The horse had been weak with a kidney infection, and was having trouble crossing the stream channels. It was swept downstream, and fell on its side, its pack filling with water. Mercer galloped his mount down the channel after the fallen horse, and was up to his saddle in water. He grabbed the halter and tried to pull the horse up, but to no avail. The horse was swept farther down the river, and Mercer gave chase. It ran aground on a shallow bar, but had even stopped trying to lift its head out of the water. Mercer finally got the animal to its feet, and brought it safely across the river.

Mercer later told me that he thought he was going to have to cut the gear loose and let the horse go to the Bering Sea. He said that he used weak rope for the pack string, so that one falling animal would not pull down the whole string. He had never lost a horse in a river, but the man he had bought out had once lost five at one time while packing for mountain climbers. Mercer assured us that none of our gear had gotten wet, since he had put his own gear on the weak horse. I replied that I had been so concerned about the horse that I had forgotten about the possibility of losing our gear.

Mercer left his pack string on a large island just beyond the river's biggest channel, then came back across the channel to give us a ride. I mounted "Major," the saddle horse belonging to Mercer's son. It was no easy task swinging up into the saddle with a 75-pound pack on my back, especially since the child-sized stirrups were too small to fit my boots. I crossed the raging channel, and hurriedly dug my camera out of the two plastic bags and the rubberized nylon bag which I had put it into before starting to wade the river. Schlichter came across next, then we both waited as Mercer went back to S. Taylor and brought him across the three channels he had not waded. The three of us then forded a relatively small, but deep channel which was nestled up against the south bank of the McKinley River. We took off our boots and dried our feet, then put on our socks. Taylor moved very slowly, putting his socks on, taking them off again, smoothing wrinkles.

Mercer went past, and said that we should try to keep up so he could help us cross Clearwater Creek, since it was no doubt much higher than it had been three days previously. Schlichter and I stood with our heavy packs, hoping that this would speed Taylor up. I asked him if he had anything wrong with his feet, and he replied no, that he was just resting. Taylor wouldn't hurry, and Mercer had already disappeared over the river bluff. The banks were much higher on this side than they had been on the north side of the river, so Schlichter and I climbed to the top of the bluff in order to see where Mercer was going. We stood at the edge of the bluff, watching Mercer getting farther and farther away to the south, and S. Taylor sitting beside the river below us, still in his bare feet. It had been cloudy most of the day, and now the sponge-like sky began to drip, so we put on our ponchos and threw them up over our packs to keep our gear dry. We had waited twenty to twenty-five minutes for Taylor, and he showed no sign of being ready to go.

Schlichter and I struck out across the boggy tundra, aiming for a small, rounded hill on the horizon, two miles away. It looked, in both color and form, much like a huge turtle, and hence its name, "Turtle Hill." Mercer disappeared behind the hill, and S. Taylor finally appeared on the top of the bluffs near the river. We met Mercer at Turtle Hill, where he had stopped for lunch. He asked if we were having any trouble keeping up. I said no, but that Taylor was moving very slowly. Schlichter walked to the top of the hill and shouted path-finding directions to Taylor. Mercer saddled up, and told us to aim toward a Florida-shaped snowbank, which was on the bank of Clearwater Creek, another three miles away across the treeless landscape.

Taylor arrived at Turtle Hill about ten minutes after Mercer had departed, and I explained to him the necessity for us to keep up with the pack string so we could be sure of getting across Clearwater Creek. We set out across the tundra at a good clip, and Taylor seemed to have no trouble maintaining the pace. The going was easy, because the tundra was level, firm, and well-drained despite the heavy rains of the last three days. Just before we reached Clearwater Creek, we flushed a red fox out of his hiding place in a hollow of the tundra, and he raced for less populated regions.

Skirting the shores of numerous small kettle lakes, we soon arrived at the high, steep bluffs overlooking Clearwater Creek and descended to the stream. We crossed the stream in style, aboard Major. After a sparse lunch (a can of sardines) we once again shouldered our packs and headed southward to our next objective, Cache Creek. The mosquitoes, which had not been bad all day, started to swarm about us now. Taylor kept up well, and we forded Cache Creek together without difficulty.

Schlichter and I climbed through the alder scrub on the creekbottom, and up to a large rock on a high terrace overlooking the valley. Here we wrung out our socks and prepared to move on up the valley. Taylor straggled up the hill to join us. After moving well for the last four miles, he was slowing down again.

The route ahead was dry and pleasant, but with considerable up-and-down stretches. We followed a tundra-covered morainal ridge until it was cut by a small stream, descended to the stream and crossed it, then climbed toward the crest of the ridge which stood 700 feet above the valley floor. From the flanks of the hill, we waved to Taylor, who was about fifty yards behind us on the other side of the stream. We saw him cross the stream and start up the hill, and we resumed our climb toward the ridgetop. As we topped the ridge and started to walk along its level crest, I looked back and saw Taylor still coming up the hill. We contoured along the ridge until we reached a point where we had to drop down 300 feet into the valley of Cache Creek. Here we stopped to wait for Taylor, since we would have been unable to see him top the ridge if we had started down. As we waited, five caribou walked past within 100 feet of us. After I had taken some pictures of the caribou, Schlichter gave a whoop, so we could see how fast a startled caribou could run.

We waited for about ten minutes for Taylor to show up, without result. Where could he be? He had been right behind us. We had visions of him sitting somewhere on the side of the moraine, resting. We decided to go back and look for him, because it was possible that he might have slipped and injured himself. We left our packs and walked back to the other side of the ridge. Taylor was nowhere to be seen. Schlichter cupped his hands megaphone style and called, "Steve!" He repeated the call several times, and from far away a faint reply reached our ears. Taylor had crossed the stream, climbed the hill on which we stood, *descended* the hill and *recrossed* the stream. He had headed up the small dead-end valley which the stream had cut in the side of the huge morainal hill.

Taylor sauntered slowly toward us, finally plopping down in a snowbank about 400 feet away. It was obvious that he wasn't coming any further, so we walked over to him. I said, "You picked kind of a wet place to sit."

"Easier for you to see me," came the reply. I asked him how he had gotten into the wrong valley, to which he replied matter-of-factly, "I just followed the trail." He had followed one of eighteen parallel caribou tracks.

I was shocked by this, still another indication of the experience level of Steve Taylor, and I commented: "There aren't any trails around here, those are caribou tracks. They aren't climbing mountains, they're after food. I hope you don't follow meltwater channels on the glacier. They go into crevasses."

We returned to where Schlichter and I had left our packs, and I proceeded to point out the entire route to Taylor so he would not become lost again. I told Taylor that we would move on toward McGonagall Pass, and perhaps camp somewhere along the way. I asked him if he wanted to start up the valley now or rest a while, and he decided that he would prefer to rest. I told him that we would stay close to Cache Creek, and he should therefore have no trouble finding us when he started moving again.

The mosquitoes were draining us dry, and I was eager to move on upward, and hopefully out of mosquito range. Schlichter and I descended to the creekbed and walked a short distance up the valley. At 23:20, we stopped to take pictures looking north at the setting sun, and south at the pink alpine glow on McGonagall and Oastler Mountains, which stand sentinel to either side of McGonagall Pass. I delayed a bit to change film, then we decided to have dinner: a can of beans. By the time our sumptuous repast was finished, we further decided that we should sleep here for a few hours before moving on. We had been on the trail for fourteen hours with 75-pound packs, and we needed the rest. We spread our sleeping bags out on the soft, dry sand of the streambed, crawled in, donned our mosquito head nets, and quickly fell asleep.

The next morning at 07:05, we continued up the valley toward McGonagall Pass, whose base was now only three miles away. Taylor had not caught up with us during the night, having spent the night on the moraine above the valley. We were sure that he would have no trouble finding the pass, because it was a sunny, clear day, and I had shown him the exact route. Also, there were no precipitous spots to cause a fall, and no rivers to be crossed. We forded the West Fork of Cache Creek, which was fifteen feet wide and less than a foot deep, and passed Mercer's camp at an elevation of 4,000 feet. We soon reached the equipment cache at 4,400 feet. The horses had been unable to go any further, because the valley narrowed abruptly and was filled with snow.

After climbing more than a mile toward the pass, we met Wilcox, McLaughlin, and Janes, who were on their way down to pick up equipment from the cache. A few minutes more brought us within sight of a ten-foot bamboo pole which was stuck in the snow on the pass, and then the tents of Camp I appeared. The tents were pitched on the edge of the level area at the summit of McGonagall Pass. The elevation at the pass was 5,720 feet. The view was exciting, looking down on the immense river of ice known as the Muldrow Glacier, and up its tiers of fractured ice to the North Peak of Mount McKinley. Ten minutes after our arrival at the pass, clouds obscured Mount McKinley. We did not see the peak again for five days.

Schlichter and I gorged ourselves on crackers, cheese, and sausages; and rested our pack-sore backs. Mercer's son and the ranch guest from Camp Denali arrived at the pass, and we visited for a while. Kurt said, "Wilcox is just doing this climb for publicity." Later, Schlichter said to me, "It sounds like he's been talking to his father." Perhaps.

Lewis was working down by the edge of the glacier, seventy vertical feet below the pass and about 200 yards away. He came up to meet us. I asked him how things had gone for the past three days. He said that the scientific work was "pure Mickey Mouse." I asked how he had liked the Wilcox group food, and he replied, "Well, there's lots of it."

Schlichter and I descended to the equipment cache to start carrying gear up to the pass. As we reached the cache, S. Taylor was just starting up the trail after a talk with Wilcox. Wilcox was angry, and he asked, "Why did you leave Steve, when there were big rivers to cross?"

I had no way of knowing what Taylor had told him, but in any case there were no rivers to cross, only one small brook. I told Wilcox that we had given Taylor complete directions, and had expected him to follow us the night before. I related how terribly slow Taylor had been, and suggested that Wilcox ask Mercer for verification. I also told of how Taylor had gotten lost following the caribou tracks, and how we had gone back for him. Wilcox said, "My only question now is whether to send you three back. It seems you're still the Colorado group."

Schlichter was moved to comment at this, asking, "Why was he the only one out of nine you left with us?"

Wilcox said that Taylor had been "feeling ill," and had requested to be left at Wonder Lake for three days. This was the first we had heard of this from any source. I told Wilcox that the Park rangers were of the opinion that Taylor was too weak experiencewise to be able to climb McKinley. Wilcox became very defensive about that issue, since he had personally pled Taylor's case with the Park Service, and gotten him back in the expedition after the Park Service had refused to grant

Taylor permission to climb. I then told Wilcox that Mercer had informed us that the first party had been spread out for a distance of over five miles, from Clearwater Creek nearly to McGonagall Pass. Schiff had been the last man, and he had been left alone, while Wilcox had been miles up the valley, third man from the front. Wilcox denied this, but it was later confirmed not only by Mercer, but by other members of the Wilcox group as well.

Wilcox's indignation was somewhat tempered by our forceful "counterattack," so he packed a load and started up toward the pass. I discussed the situation with Schlichter, and we both appreciated the position Wilcox was in as leader of the group. We caught up with Wilcox and Taylor, and I said that I was sorry for any consternation I might have caused them. Taylor said he had no ill feelings, and Wilcox seemed satisfied.

We had been on the trail only one day, and already had engaged in a serious argument with Wilcox. It did not seem to be a good omen. As it turned out, however, it was our first and only verbal clash with Wilcox, though not the last within his original group.

McGonagall Pass was the second demarcation point. Its narrow crest divided the life of the green valleys from the sterility of ice and rock. Mercer went back to Wonder Lake, and we were alone. Our only contact with the outside world would be by radio. Lines of support were now cut, the expedition would succeed or fail as determined by its luck, pluck, and strength.

᠎᠎᠎᠎᠎᠎᠎᠎᠎ **4** ᠎᠎᠎᠎᠎᠎᠎᠎᠎

THE MULDROW GLACIER
At the Giant's Feet

Camp I commanded a magnificent view from its location on McGonagall Pass. The Muldrow Glacier tumbles down from the heights of Mount McKinley, and grinds slowly by the foot of the pass. Just across the Muldrow from the pass is the glacier-covered face of Mount Tatum, a chaos of shattered ice. The Traleika Glacier, as large as the Muldrow itself, joins the Muldrow at the foot of Mount Tatum. We could see up the Muldrow as far as the Lower Icefall, where a rising turn obscured the upper glacier from our view.

The Muldrow is confined by steep ridges on both sides. Until we reached Denali Pass at 18,200 feet, we would either be climbing on the glacier between these ridges, or on the crest of the southeastern ridge. McGonagall Pass is a gap in the northwestern ridge, which in its upper reaches is called "Pioneer Ridge." This ridge forms one wall of the Muldrow and Harper Glaciers all the way to their source at Denali Pass. It culminates in the North Peak of Mount McKinley, at 19,470 feet. On the other side of the Muldrow, the southeastern ridge begins on Mount Tatum, and proceeds up the face of Mount McKinley. It includes the summits of Mount Carpé and Mount Koven, and the important section of the route known as Karstens Ridge. Its culmination point was our goal: the 20,320-foot South Peak of Mount McKinley.

Continual rain and fog made our life at McGonagall Pass an amphibious one. Clothes became soaked while on the trail, and tent floors were small swimming pools. Any break in the clouds was a signal to spread things out to dry. W. Taylor encouraged the sun: "C'mon Sun! Show us you haven't forgotten your chillun!" He suggested that we should go around naked to show our faith in the Sun God.

The twenty-fourth of June was a day of multiple activities, tying up the last details of the scientific work as well as making the first foray upglacier toward the Lower Icefall of the Muldrow Glacier. Clark led the first actual climbing party, including Luchterhand, Russell, and W. Taylor. The advance team was charged with finding the route, marking it with four-foot bamboo wands, and locating Camp II as near the base of the Lower Icefall as they could.

Some of us spent the day relaying loads from the cache where Mercer had unloaded the horses. Between relays, we searched the glacier for the advance team, and marked their progress. They covered the first one and a half miles fairly quickly, and then disappeared behind a large transverse moraine which crossed the glacier's entire width. Hours later they were visible again, near Gunsight Pass, seemingly not moving at all. Distances were deceiving however, because the glacier was generally featureless and level up to the foot of the Lower Icefall. The advance team was actually four and a half miles away, and viewed from this distance their movement looked slow indeed.

Upon the return of the advance team in the evening, W. Taylor was asked if there was a water supply at the site selected for Camp II, or if we would have to melt snow. "There's plenty of water up there," he replied. "We'll be pouring it out of our tents."

On one of the relays from the cache, I had carried a two-gallon plastic can of kerosene in my pack. The can had leaked, and a dark, oily stain covered the bottom of the pack. W. Taylor said he was glad they were using gasoline instead of kerosene. Lewis replied, "But ours feels nicer." He was referring to the slickness of kerosene. We had chosen kerosene stoves because they were much more economical of fuel than were gasoline stoves. We were not to be disappointed; our fuel use proved to be even more economical than we had expected.

After dinner, Russell discussed with me his plan to split the expedition into two summit parties. He suggested that the strongest team should make the summit climb one or two days before the rest of the men. He had no particular reason for his suggestion. Different circumstances might dictate different courses of action, but I told Russell that I would oppose splitting the party unless there was a definite advantage in doing so. In any event, it was too early to start planning the summit assault teams now. Russell also told me that he thought we should cache both Colorado group stoves here at McGonagall Pass, and at least one of the Wilcox group's four stoves. He also wanted to leave all of the snow shovel handles at McGonagall Pass, and use ice axes as shovel handles. Wilcox agreed to leaving the shovel handles behind, but I did not. Consequently, the Colorado group's shovel was in demand at every camp, since it was the only one with a handle.

The entire party, in three ropes of four each, carried loads to Camp II on 25 June. The glacier was virtually level, and the walking was so monotonous that it seemed we got farther from McGonagall Pass without getting closer to Camp II.

During our drive through British Columbia and the Yukon, Lewis had several times pointed out locations that he thought were capable of producing a good wheat crop. As we crossed the transverse moraine in the middle of the Muldrow Glacier, Schlichter saw opportunity in its boulders and pulverized rock: "This looks like pretty good land for wheat."

We encountered no crevasses in the four and a half miles from Camp I to Camp II. Two suspicious sags were probed, but both were solid. A sudden left turn in the trail signaled our nearness to the camp, and soon after we saw the orange plastic sheet covering the cache, and the probe pole standing beside it.

Camp II was situated on a slightly upthrown block of bare ice, contrasting with the level snow-covered terrain around it. The ice block was a remnant of the crevasses and ogives of the Lower Icefall. The elevation of Camp II was 6,500 feet. One-half mile upglacier lay the gaping crevasses of the Lower Icefall, while off to the southeast side of the glacier loomed the summit of Mount Tatum. Tatum provided Camp II with a dramatic backdrop of tortured ice, ravaged by numerous icefalls and crevasses. On the other side of the glacier, to the northwest, was a low gap in the ridge, less than 100 feet higher than our camp. The gap was Gunsight Pass, the last exit from this glacial highway to the sky.

A small pond was in the depression just upglacier from our little ice hill, and it was to serve as our water supply. We found several unused butane stove cartridges on the ice, which indicated that this point had been higher than the surrounding glacier for at least two years, and had been used as a cache site by some previous expedition. The camp had been thoroughly probed as a precaution against hidden crevasses, and the probed perimeter was wanded. No one was to leave the wanded enclosure unless he was roped up.

My rope of four, including Schlichter, Lewis, and W. Taylor, made the return trip to Camp I at almost a run. Speed was one way to alleviate monotony, and it was made possible by our now-empty packs.

It was rainy and cold on the morning of the twenty-sixth until about 10:00. Then the sun shone on the pass for the first time in days, and damp equipment blossomed forth on every rock around the camp. One hour later a dense cloud rushed into the camp, pouring right through McGonagall Pass. A silent movies type chase ensued, as we all scrambled to get our semi-dried gear under cover. The fog gave way to snow, the first that we had encountered on the climb.

Wilcox called a meeting in the driving snow, to discuss the use of skis by McLaughlin and Clark. This donnybrook made our confrontation with Wilcox three days earlier look mild by comparison. Both Clark and McLaughlin were experienced ski mountaineers, and they had requested Wilcox's permission to form a rope of two on return trips from Camp II, thus enabling them to use the speed advantage of their skis. Wilcox refused, and called the meeting to impress his decision upon the whole group.

Wilcox said he would allow no "downhill skiing" on this climb, and that he had made this clear before the trip. Clark observed that 900 vertical feet in four and one-half miles was hardly downhill skiing. He also pointed out that he and McLaughlin had far more extensive skiing and ski-mountaineering experience than did Wilcox, and were therefore more qualified to make a judgment concerning the use of skis. This questioning of his judgment angered Wilcox, so he proceeded to put further restrictions on the use of skis: No rope may have more than one skier on it, since a skier could not hold a crevasse fall as well as a man on snowshoes could, and was limited in the application of an ice ax arrest.

Clark and McLaughlin countered strongly (and correctly) that a skier could hold a fall by edging with his skis much better than a man with snowshoes could, and could handle an ax just as well. Besides, no crevasses had been found on the trail between Camps I and II.

Wilcox leveled his strongest threat at the two skiers: "We'll do it safely or we won't do it at all. If any of you don't want to follow my orders, you can just take your share of the food and pack out and do Logan or something." S. Taylor had said at Wonder Lake that if we did McKinley quickly and had food left over, maybe we should do Logan on the way home, an idea that he most likely got from Wilcox. This casual reference to the Yukon's 19,850-foot Mount Logan showed a disturbing lack of knowledge. Logan is a far more difficult and isolated adversary than is Mount McKinley.

Wilcox had by now threatened to send half of the party back to Wonder Lake, including the deputy leader, and I feared the situation was approaching an explosion point. Schlichter, Lewis, and I were all huddled under Schlichter's poncho, to keep out of the snow. The group was cold and wet, and as a move to break the impasse and get us out of the snow, I joked: "Tell you what, Joe. You take one skier on your rope and I'll take all the rest of 'em on mine." There were only two skiers in the entire team. The small attempt at humor worked, and Wilcox relaxed a little.

Wilcox asked if there were any more complaints. W. Taylor said, "I didn't have any until you called this meeting. Now I'm soaked." The group laughed and nodded in agreement, and the meeting was adjourned.

Wilcox came to my tent and informed me that I had been selected to find the route past the first obstacle on the Muldrow Glacier, the Lower Icefall. My climbing team had also been chosen for me, including Lewis, McLaughlin, and S. Taylor. We were instructed to pack our personal gear for a carry to Camp II.

Eight of us prepared to carry equipment to Camp II, selecting our loads from the food and equipment cache. W. Taylor noticed that only one of the Wilcox group's one-day food bags was gone from the cache. Two one-day bags or one two-day bag constituted a full load, so someone was carrying a half load. Taylor yelled at Schiff, who was just leaving camp for the edge of the glacier: "Come back here Anshel, you rascal!" Schiff came back, the picture of innocence, and Taylor good-naturedly told him to pack a full load. Reluctantly, Schiff complied.

We traveled to Camp II in two four-man ropes. My rope included Lewis, Russell, and W. Taylor. Clark led the other rope, with S. Taylor, McLaughlin, and Schiff. As the four men who were not on the advance team prepared to return to Camp I, Russell said, "I refuse to climb on the same rope with Jerry Clark." He was still angry with Clark because of the ski-use argument.

Clark attempted to reason with Russell, but to no avail. Clark then said: "As deputy leader of the expedition, I have no choice but to order you to remain here. We can't have you going unroped on the glacier."

Schiff tried to talk some sense into Russell, but without success. W. Taylor's face mirrored his astonishment at the situation. "C'mon gentlemen, let's do it!" Taylor exclaimed. "I'm getting cold!" Russell was adamant. Finally, Clark and Schiff went on one rope, while W. Taylor took Russell on another rope.

The four of us in the advance team were now alone, the first group to camp on the glacier. I surveyed the route ahead for tomorrow's climb. The map indicated relatively few crevasses on the left (southeast) side of the Lower Icefall, but we could see a great number of them. The right (northwest) side of the icefall was severely broken also, but Washburn's guide had said that the right side was usually easier to force than the left. Two small hanging glaciers on the valley wall presented the major danger on the right side, whereas the valley wall on the left was a massive, snow-covered avalanche slope.

As I stood studying the icefall, a muffled crack and rumble emanated from high on the shoulders of Mount Tatum, on the left side of the glacier. The roar grew more intense, and a stream of snow mixed with rock became visible, flowing, leaping, cascading down the mountainside. By the time the avalanche reached the Muldrow Glacier, it was a gray mass of homogenized debris. It slid far out onto the left side of the Lower Icefall, an ugly gray slash across the white snow. Our route was chosen. We would go to the right.

The sky was of leaden hue the next morning, the twenty-seventh of June. The gaping crevasses of the Lower Icefall looked even more sinister through the mist. I put Lewis behind me on the rope, to hold me in case I fell into a covered crevasse while routefinding. S. Taylor was placed third on the rope, and McLaughlin was anchor man. We encountered our first crevasses on the flat stretch of glacier above camp, and they became more numerous as we approached the base of the icefall. I continually probed in front of my snowshoes with my ice ax, seeking covered crevasses. I found a small one on the side of a little ice hump, and knocked a hole in its snow cover so that it could be seen and avoided.

My snowshoe binding had worked loose, so I stopped on top of the ice hump to tighten it. I told Lewis to move up carefully, and to watch out for the crevasse. I finished tightening my snowshoes, and looked down at Lewis as he stood at the edge of the crevasse. Suddenly he tipped over sideways and vanished into the glacier. He had fallen into a large crevasse while probing the small one I had uncovered. I fell immediately into an ax arrest. I jammed the pick as far as it would go into the solid ice of the little hill. The pick penetrated only about one inch, a tenuous arrest at best. To provide a static belay point, I wrapped the rope around the adze of my ax and knelt on the shaft to hold the ax in place. I told S. Taylor to carefully cross the crevasse and come up to me, so he could take over the belay and free me to pull Lewis out of the crevasse. Taylor established an ax belay and held it while I placed two ice screws. I clipped them into a prussik sling which had been attached to the climbing rope holding Lewis.

McLaughlin had taken up slack, and held Lewis from the other end of the rope. I could not see Lewis from my position on top of the ice hill, but I could hear his voice echoing up from the crevasse as though from a cave. Lewis kept asking, "Do you have me?! Do you have me?!", because as the rope stretched or cut into the lip of the crevasse, it allowed him to move down an inch or so. To him of course, an inch felt like a foot. Lewis asked how far down he was, since he was wedged in horizontally, face down, and could not see upward.

I moved down to the lower edge of the crevasse and looked in. Lewis was about nine feet down. I asked him if he was all right. "Hell no, I'm not all right!!" I smiled and relaxed a little. The vehemence of his reply indicated that he was uninjured. As we worked on the lip of the crevasse, small amounts of snow were unavoidably knocked down on Lewis' back. "Don't knock snow on me!" he called out. There was a definite tone of anxiety in his voice. Still unable to look upward, he was forced to contemplate the depths of the crevasse, and he feared that we were about to bury him in a deluge of snow. After tugging Lewis into an upright position, McLaughlin and I lowered the end of the climbing rope to him and hoisted his pack out of the crevasse. Lewis then handed his ax up to us, and we lowered a pulley for him to clip into his waist loop.

McLaughlin, standing on his skis, served as the tie-off anchor for the pulley. We pulled a very relieved Lewis out of the crevasse. As his nerves quieted, his natural sense for beauty and his conditioned sense of the photographer returned. "I wish there was enough light down there to take pictures. It was all subtle shades of blue." The crevasse's superficial expression had been small, but Lewis said that it opened up underneath into a cavern big enough to play basketball in, and contained a lake.

Although Lewis knew that our ⅜" nylon rope was plenty strong, its small size was not psychologically reassuring when he was dangling in the crevasse. He said, "The next rope I buy is going to be an inch thick!"

I told Lewis later that day, "Jerry, I was the second happiest person on the glacier when we pulled you out of that crevasse."

At the base of the icefall we cut to the right and got off the glacier. I picked a route which cut across the toes of the avalanche cones which were at the base of the valley wall. We continued along the avalanche cones, avoiding the crevasses of the Lower Icefall, until we reached the top of the icefall at an elevation of 7,300 feet. We resumed travel on the glacier, but had gone only a few yards before whiteout conditions caused us to halt at the edge of a large crevasse. There appeared to be a way around it on the left, toward the center of the glacier, but we could not be sure under these visibility conditions.

I marked the end of our trail with three wands, and we returned to the edge of the glacier. We had covered only one and a half miles, and 800 vertical feet, but we had surmounted the Lower Icefall, and the route had looked unobstructed on to the Hill of Cracks before the mist closed in. We constructed a cache behind a large schist boulder, and left our high-altitude boots and down clothing, crampons, and a spool of water-ski tow rope which was to be used as fixed line on Karstens Ridge.

We started down our trail across the avalanche cones, pausing at 19:00 for a radio contact with the party at Camp I. We established a new route on the descent, continuing down the side of the glacier until we were almost even with Camp II, and then cutting directly across the glacier to camp. This route avoided all of the crevasses at the base of the Lower Icefall.

Wilcox's rope arrived in Camp II shortly after we did, heavily laden with equipment from Camp I. They set up their tents, and Wilcox proceeded to prepare dinner. He overprimed the stove, and gasoline spread across the tent floor. He lit the stove, and the floor burst into flame. Wilcox managed to smother the fire before any damage was done. When the last rope arrived in Camp II, they were told by Russell that, "Our Fearless Leader tried to burn down the tent."

Clark's rope arrived more than an hour after Wilcox's, having made an exceptionally slow trip from Camp I. We had watched them from Camp II, sitting motionless along the trail for ten to fifteen minutes at a time. Schlichter later told me that Clark had stopped repeatedly to adjust his skis. He had waxed his skis, then stopped to remove the wax, stopped again to put on his climbing skins, then to take them off. The men had been carrying their heaviest loads yet, and Clark's physical condition was starting to make itself evident.

That night, as we were squirming into our sleeping bags, Schlichter asked me why I was sleeping fully clothed, except for my boots. I replied, "I'm practicing for the high mountain."

Late the next morning, on 28 June, Wilcox selected a team to push the trail on toward the Hill of Cracks, which lay three and a half miles away, and 1,575 feet higher than Camp II. The team was composed of Wilcox, Janes, Russell, and Luchterhand. Due to Lewis's experience with the crevasse on the previous day, it was advised that everyone carry an ice screw where it could be reached easily, for use as an anchor. W. Taylor turned an ice screw over in his hand and asked, "How do you use this thing? Screw it in, or hammer it in, or what?" Here we were on the biggest ice mountain in North America, and Taylor had never seen an ice screw.

Wilcox departed with his rope, but Clark did not like the idea of starting out in the middle of the day to pass beneath the avalanche slopes at the edge of the glacier. I agreed, and suggested that we wait until nightfall to make our carry, especially since we had received several inches of new snow the night before, snow which was now poised to avalanche in the midday heat.

Wilcox radioed back from the top of the Lower Icefall, informing us that he had put up a new route through the icefall, preferring crevasses to avalanche cones. Wilcox's rope arrived in camp about 22:00, as the rest of us were preparing loads for a carry to the site they had selected for Camp III. While Wilcox's team was just outside camp, Russell shouted, "Who put up that suicide route over the avalanches?!" He knew very well who had put up the route. Russell continued, "Joe put up a beautiful route on the edge of the glacier, through the crevasses. A beautiful route." A little over a week later, when the Mountaineering Club of Alaska Expedition reached the Lower Icefall, they saw both routes. They picked the one over the toes of the avalanche cones.

The advance team had made it as far as the top of the Hill of Cracks, to an elevation of 8,075 feet. Wilcox said they had turned back "about 500 feet" from the proposed campsite due to a whiteout. They had dumped their loads at their point of furthest progress, covered the cache with orange plastic, and left the probe pole at the cache. This day's climb had been Luchterhand's first encounter with big crevasses, and he was duly impressed. "It's colder than a witch's heart up there. That's the land of perpetual ice and snow. That Hill of Cracks is full of cracks, big mothahs. We crossed lots of them over a hundred feet deep."

Russell said he had fallen into crevasses three times (only part way, presumably), and Janes had fallen once. Referring to Luchterhand, who was wearing large trail snowshoes rather than Snowtreads, Russell said, "He'd just glide over them [the crevasses] on those big snowshoes, and I'd break through."

Luchterhand replied, "Damn right, I'm going to wear my nice big snowshoes all the time."

All of the talk about "huge" crevasses, and falls into crevasses, made the second party apprehensive about the Hill of Cracks. The advance team headed for supper and the sack, and the remaining eight of us prepared to start up the trail. I asked Clark if we were going to take a radio along, since I had not seen him put it in his pack. "No," he replied. "We have two-thirds of the party. I'm sure we could handle anything that might come up."

S. Taylor had put on his face mask and goggles, probably due to the scare talk about the cold on the Hill of Cracks. It was not really cold enough for a face mask, and goggles were not necessary at the time because the sun was down. W. Taylor looked at S. Taylor and laughed: "If they find the body they'll never believe it."

We left Camp II at 22:30, and greeted 29 June while laboring through the Lower Icefall. We followed the route Wilcox had put up, running through the crevasses at the right edge of the icefall, generally about 75 to 100 feet from the original route at the foot of the avalanche cones. The most difficult section was at the base of the icefall, where a couple of steeply ascending turns had to be negotiated, a hard task with a 65-pound pack. The first of these pitches was about ten feet high and very icy, allowing almost no purchase for snowshoes. The route crossed several flimsy bridges, one of which was especially thin. This bridge collected several leg-punched holes before we were through with it. We always tiptoed gingerly across the bridge, and I was surprised that it held up, considering the many holes we knocked through it.

Near the top of the Lower Icefall, the crevasses ran all the way to the edge of the glacier, and Wilcox's route cut to the right to avoid the steep, unbridged crevasses. To get off the glacier, the route went over an open crevasse which had to be jumped, then ascended a steep, narrow bridge across a deep crevasse. The bridge was weak, and its steepness and narrowness made a fall very possible. It could have been easily bypassed by going ten feet farther off the glacier, a modification which we made on our return from the Hill of Cracks. Above this bridge, the new route joined the old one, and skirted the upper portion of the Lower Icefall.

We stopped at the top of the icefall to pick up the gear we had cached on the twenty-seventh. Clark was not pleased with the new route through the Lower Icefall, and he said to me, "I can see there's something to be said for the other route. This route isn't all they played it up to be."

The sun was just coming up, a diffused glow shining through the mist and the light snow which had begun falling. The Hill of Cracks had received such tremendous advance billing that none of us was eager to dash off into the gathering whiteout. However, our rope did not want to try to outwait Clark's team, so we started up the glacier.

We crossed a snow bridge over the big crevasse which had marked our point of furthest progress on the twenty-seventh, and cut sharply to the left to make an end run around some more large crevasses. We plodded up the center of the glacier on the flat which lies above the Lower Icefall, grinding off the mile to the base of the Hill of Cracks. We started up the Hill of Cracks, and McLaughlin started calling out, "A little slower," at intervals, and finally began calling for rest stops. Short rest stops are fine, but prolonged stops were later to become a problem and a potential danger on the climb.

The fog thickened, and we were able to see nothing except each other and the orange-flagged wands marking the trail ahead. We could see two wands at a time, which indicated a visibility of about 300 feet. The Hill of Cracks was rent by huge crevasses, but did not have the menacing seracs and ice cliffs of an icefall. As we approached the top of the Hill of Cracks, we could see crevasses yawning on either side of us. We crossed two bridged crevasses at right angles to each other, the second one of which had a hole punched in the bridge. After proceeding a few more feet along the trail, I spotted the probe pole sticking in the snow. I shouted that I could see the cache, and our pace picked up slightly. The right angle crevasses therafter served as a sign that we were nearing Camp III, during our tedious equipment relays between Camps II and III.

Upon reaching the cache, I probed the area so that we could all come up and dump our loads. I strained to see the route ahead, but the fog would not relent. I wanted to go on and set up Camp III, but we could not see the glacier above us. Clark and McLaughlin wanted to go back to Camp II.

During a momentary thinning of the clouds, I consulted my map and was able to identify a black triangular cliff ahead of us. It was one which Washburn had mentioned in his guide. The fog approached the whiteout stage, so we dumped our loads and started down the trail at 03:15.

We made good time, but it was like walking in a dream, just following the man ahead, able to see no landmarks due to the fog. In the still air, I could feel my breath flowing down my chin in rhythmic waves. It felt almost solid; warm and damp on cold, dry skin. The snow started falling heavily when we reached the top of the Lower Icefall, and it was still snowing hard when we reached Camp II at 04:50. Clark's party unroped and let the rope fall where it may, a habit the Wilcox group had started at the glacier's edge at Camp I. I took the extra few minutes necessary to coil my rope and store it in the cache, then crawled into the tent to get some sleep.

The falling snow brought out a playful streak in some of the men. Schiff made a snowball with the new, wet snow, and threw it at the tent occupied by Russell and Luchterhand. It was on target, and from inside the tent Luchterhand roared, "Cut that out, you mothah!" Walt Taylor looked stunned, then patted Schiff on the back and said, "I didn't know you had it in you, you old rascal." Taylor suggested that we have a game of fox and geese, and even stomped out a course in the snow, but could find no takers.

The snowstorm continued all day on the twenty-ninth, while we slept, ate, and discussed whether or not we would rather be home watching television if we had but to wish to make it so.

The storm broke on the morning of 30 June, leaving us with a crystal clear, warm day—and three feet of new snow. The Wilcox group had to drag the snow with their ice axes to find the ropes they had dropped when they unroped on the morning of 29 June. We spent the day cleaning ourselves and our gear; drying out sleeping bags, foam pads, and shell parkas; and taking pictures. Schlichter and I had not worn high socks in our rubber boots, and we paid for the oversight, spending part of the morning cleansing and bandaging the raw sores which the boot tops had sawed into our calves.

The glacier was ablaze with light, and hardly a cloud was to be seen. The storm had covered every surface that could conceivably hold snow, as well as a few that couldn't, resulting in a blinding concentration of light on the valley floor. The valley walls reflected sunlight onto the glacier, which in turn reflected the light upward. We were living and working in a gargantuan reflector oven, enabling us to walk about very comfortably in our net underwear or short pants.

We packed loads to be carried to Camp III that night. Wilcox had designated himself, Schiff, Janes, and Schlichter as the advance team for work above Camp III. The advance team was to establish Camp III and put up a route past the Great Icefall.

The entire party of twelve started for Camp III at nearly midnight. Luchterhand led the first rope, to break trail with his large trail snowshoes. I led the third rope, which left Camp II at 23:40. The month of July tiptoed silently up behind our backs and overtook us as we approached the Lower Icefall. It brought with it the rising sun, as the low, broken clouds on the northern horizon took on the blush of dawn. Mount McKinley loomed at the head of the glacier, a blue-white giant still sulking in the shadow of night. A look down the Muldrow Glacier revealed the northern sky growing brighter, and in the opposite direction the mountain started to take on the hint of a pink glow. McKinley has many aspects, and for three hours we were treated to a kaleidoscopic display of nature's finest mountain moods.

The sky downglacier turned orange, the peak upglacier became a

brilliant, glowing pink, standing bright and clear against the dark blue
sky. The color shades changed with every passing moment. I had seen
only one sight to compare with it; France's Mont Blanc glowing pink
in the sunrise with the full moon setting directly on the summit.

I watched the scene largely through my camera viewfinder, ex-
claiming, "Beautiful! Beautiful! This is what I climb mountains for!"
The mountain changed from pink to gold as the sun broke above the
clouds on the horizon. The flat above the Lower Icefall looked like a
scene from the Arabian Nights, with a caravan of climbers crossing the
undulating golden dunes of the crevassed glacier. As the sun rose
higher, the peak's golden tone faded slowly, to be replaced by its natural white color.

Russell was second on Luchterhand's rope, and instead of following
Luchterhand's track he once made a parallel track about thirty feet
long. The rope's third man, Walt Taylor, inscribed this warning on the
island of snow between the two tracks: "Do not cross median."

Luchterhand's rope had pulled ahead of the other two ropes, which
were delayed due to Schiff's difficulties with his snowshoe bindings.
We caught up with the lead team at the base of the Hill of Cracks,
where they had stopped for a rest. Luchterhand was tired, justifiably
so, since he had been breaking trail in the new snow for nearly three
miles. His rope had been stopped for a few minutes when we caught
up with them, and we waited for another ten to fifteen minutes.

The peak ahead of us and the mountain walls behind us were blazing with the purest of white light. The only shade to be seen anywhere
was beneath the cornices on the ridgetops, or beside the ice blocks on
the shattered glacier faces. By contrast with the world of white, the
shadows appeared to have a greenish hue. This coloration was likely an
optical illusion. As we surveyed the breathtaking panorama around us,
an avalanche roared down the slopes of Mt. Carpé, just above us. The
avalanche slid and leaped, showering down onto the Muldrow with a
rolling thunder that belied its feathery appearance.

Schlichter, Lewis, and I were getting painfully chilled feet, because
the snow was bitterly cold, even though the sun was bright. We
stomped our feet and wiggled our toes, trying to keep the circulation
going. Occasional rest stops of short duration are beneficial, but after

five minutes the effects of a stop are more bad than good. Long stops cause a slowing of circulation and chilling of the body, especially if a person has been perspiring; muscles cool and tighten; the will to continue sometimes diminishes; and time is lost, time which may later prove to be valuable beyond any price. Later in the day, Lewis and I discussed the long delay on the trail, and agreed that we could not endure such lengthy delays without risking frostbitten feet.

We reached the top of the Hill of Cracks, and I stopped my rope at the cache to pick up some of the gear we had dumped there two days before. I looked upglacier and noticed that the first two ropes had stopped, just one rope length up the trail from the cache. I assumed that Wilcox had decided to locate Camp III here, at 8,075 feet, instead of pushing on to Washburn's recommended site at 8,600 feet. Russell was unroped, standing with his arms akimbo, glaring at Clark. We were too far away to be able to hear what they were saying to one another. Wilcox probed the campsite, and we moved in to dump our loads.

The site of Camp II was just to the left (southeast) of the huge crevasses which split the top of the Hill of Cracks. Like rows of Napoleonic soldiers, the crevasses marched from the base of the black, triangular cliff on the northwest side of the glacier. The crevasses were the biggest we had seen yet, hundreds of feet long and of unknown depth. Camp III was squeezed in between two of them. We contained our curiosity regarding their depth.

Schlichter unroped, to stay in Camp III with the advance team, and Clark took his place on our rope for the return to Camp II. After we had started down the trail, I asked Clark what the problem had been with Russell. He said that Russell had unroped as soon as Wilcox had announced that this would be the site of Camp III. Clark had said, "Don't unrope, John, the area hasn't been probed yet." Russell had just leveled a withering stare at Clark.

The going was easy and pleasant on the trip back to Camp II. By the time we reached the top of the Lower Icefall, the brilliant sun had rekindled the reflector oven, causing us to shed stocking caps and shell parkas. We reached Camp II, and spent the day resting and eating.

Clark and McLaughlin had decided that they wanted to make no more long and arduous climbs such as Mount McKinley. McLaughlin said, "We'll stick to one-day climbs from now on." Late in the evening we arranged our personal gear for the move up to Camp III.

Early the next morning, 2 July, we struck camp, packed our loads, and put all remaining gear in the cache. We counted the loads remaining to be carried, and found that one more trip by the eight of us should finish the carries from Camp II. The trail between Camps II and III was by now very familiar to us, and we were able to set a good pace. We had to stop along the trail once because McLaughlin was ill, which he said was a result of the Wilcox group's chili menu.

While we were stopped on the trail, the second rope passed us. Luchterhand was last on the rope, and was being dragged up a slope while the others on his rope were on a level stretch. He bellowed, "All right you mothahs, slow it down! I'm still going uphill you know!"

I asked, "How do you like being pulled up the hills, Denny?"

"I don't mind running up them as much as I mind creeping down the other side." During our carries between Camps II and III, I had received complaints from the last man on my rope concerning my uphill-downhill pace, so I was familiar with the problem.

Even with the delay, we reached Camp III in just under four hours. Lewis and I were anxious to go back for another load, to be done with Camp II. Our work days had generally been four to six hours long, which was by no means overdoing things. I asked W. Taylor if he wanted to go back for a second load. He facetiously answered, "Sure. Who else wants to make another carry today?" Lewis said that he would go, so Taylor continued, "All right gentlemen, we need one more. Who wants to go?" There were no volunteers forthcoming. Taylor turned to me and said, "You had me worried there. I was afraid we might get a fourth man. I was just joking, you know." I knew.

Wilcox had made a rule that a four-man rope could travel alone on the glacier, but any smaller rope could not climb alone. Thus prevented from making a second trip to Camp II, we set to work enlarging Camp III. By this stage of the expedition we had our camp set-up routine well organized. The equipment cache had already been established, and the campsite had been probed for crevasses and the perimeter wanded. A latrine area had also been designated. The next task was to dig out and pack a level platform for each tent. This done, Lewis and I set up our tent, using snowshoes, ice axes, ski poles, a snowshovel, and empty butter cans to serve as tent stakes. The Wilcox group had aluminum "coolie hats," which McLaughlin had constructed for use as tent stakes.

Camp III was the first camp with no supply of liquid water, so Lewis and I started up our stoves to melt snow, and began cooking breakfast. Colorado group meals were composed of low-weight, low-bulk items. The main dishes were freeze-dried foods, which proved to be excellent. Despite their low dried weight, the meals were immense when reconstituted with water. The food was extremely high in calories, providing tasty and completely filling meals. Breakfast on the second of July consisted of hot cereal with milk and sugar, scrambled eggs with diced ham, one cup of Ovaltine, one quart of orange drink, prunes, Triscuit crackers, plum jelly, honey, and butter. Lunch included sausage, fig newtons, one quart of cherry drink, cheese, raisins, English walnuts, a candy bar, and a roll of sour fruit candies.

In both our breakfast and dinner menus, the manufacturer's suggested one-man portion of the freeze-dried foods was doubled. Dinner for the night of the second consisted of Swiss steak with thick gravy, vegetable beef soup with added bouillon, green peas, mashed potatoes, tea, Ovaltine, freeze-dried strawberries, Logan bread, Jello, peanuts, and a candy bar. We also had a variety of condiments, including jelly, butter, honey, sugar, salt, and pepper, all topped off with a vitamin pill. The Colorado group had three basic breakfast and dinner menus, although great care had been taken to ensure that no two day's menus were ever precisely the same, thus putting some variety in our diets.

At Camps I and II, the latrine areas had been what might be referred to as "unimproved." W. Taylor spent the day of 2 July building a castle-like latrine at Camp III, complete with flag-bedecked turrets. It was hailed by all as a practical accomplishment and an artistic success.

At mid-morning, Russell was outside melting snow on one of the stoves. I heard the "whump!" of a gas explosion, and looked up to see the stove in flames. Russell had overpumped the stove and the pressure had blown out the leather gasket. Russell said that stove gaskets were no good: "I always have trouble with them."

The advance team returned around midday. They had found a route through the Great Icefall. The icefall was separated lengthwise into two sections, and the route went up the middle of the glacier, near the edge of the very disturbed eastern half of the icefall. The advance team had reached a point on the glacier opposite the northeast ridge of Taylor Spur. Here they had established what we referred to as the Flatiron cache, at an elevation of about 10,600 feet. Schiff had been unable to carry his full load, and Schlichter had taken part of it for him. "I didn't mind carrying it," Schlichter told me, "except that he kept looking back at me with a big grin."

Eight of us left Camp III at 23:43, to pick up the last loads at Camp II. The clouds hovered low over the glacier, and light snowfall began just after midnight. As we plodded along on the foggy, monotonous flat between the Hill of Cracks and the Lower Icefall, Walt Taylor told us how he had visualized the climb before it started: "Climbing up a steep ridge with the sun at my back and the blue ice chips a-flyin'."

We took less than one and a half hours to reach Camp II, and quickly loaded up our packs. The plastic and paper trash around the camp was gathered up to be burned, including some packages of fruit drink powder. I suggested that it might be best to save or at least cache the drink mixes, but was told, "Nobody wants that stuff anyway." As the group stood by the flickering fire, I stepped back a few feet and watched the scene.

The sky was heavily overcast, and the sun was not visible at all. The time was 01:25. There were eight of us here, and yet I felt a deep sense of loneliness, a feeling of being really isolated for the first time on the trip. I could see McGonagall Pass, an easy two-hour walk down the glacier. It was the last vestige of the lowlands, and it would be out of sight before we reached Camp III. The expedition was now alone, a micro-civilization in a world of ice.

We left Camp II at 01:30 on 3 July, for what was to be the most tedious three and a half miles I have ever endured. Russell was leading the first rope, including Luchterhand, W. Taylor, and Lewis. I was leading the second rope, with Clark, McLaughlin, and S. Taylor. As soon as we reached the crevasses of the Lower Icefall, the first rope started to pull ahead. McLaughlin was having great difficulty negotiating the steep turns with skis, but he would not switch to his snowshoes. McLaughlin took five minutes of falling and floundering to top one pitch that I had passed in ten seconds. We finally surmounted the Lower Icefall, and started across the flat toward the Hill of Cracks. The first rope had pulled far ahead, and was nearing 7,900 feet on the Hill of Cracks while we were still laboring across the flat at about 7,550 feet.

Clark kept telling me, "Slow down! Go slower!" while I was moving as slowly as I could without stopping. To have gone any slower I either would have had to stop altogether or stand like a stork between steps, with one foot suspended in the air. We took some short rest stops, but Clark still called for a slower pace. Finally, Clark said, "I've just got to stop," then he intentionally fell over on his back, driving his pack into the snow. Clark sprawled there in the snow, resting on his pack, then McLaughlin and S. Taylor sat down. I stood, with my pack on, as I always did during rest stops. I found it less trouble to stand with a loaded pack than to take off the pack, sit in the cold snow, and then wrestle the pack back on.

Due to the fog and the snow, the scene had an unreal lighting effect. Distances faded in the unshadowed light, and it seemed we were in a dense fog. But we could see the first rope over a half mile away, so the fog was actually not very dense. The effect was due to the uniform whiteness of ground and sky, which gave no indication of the difference between feet and miles. We had been immobile for about ten minutes when we heard a rumbling on the slopes of Mount Carpé, on the south side of the glacier. A billowing avalanche became visible through the fog, growing ever larger as it swept down the mountainside directly toward us. It would have been futile to try to outrun the avalanche, especially since three of the men on our rope were fixed like rocks on the ground. I quickly surveyed the area around us, and saw that there were no avalanche tracks visible. I also knew that there was a large trench at the edge of the glacier, between us and the avalanche, and that we were about a half mile from the base of the avalanche slope. The roar increased, and the cloud loomed higher and larger. It was the biggest avalanche we had seen so far.

After the avalanche had come to a stop, I asked the others if they were ready to move on. Clark said, "Yes, but let's go slow."

I had been worried about the slow pace on the trail for several days, so I took this opportunity to express my fears: "Jerry, on this mountain, speed is safety. If you go so slowly that you get caught out in the open between camps by a bad storm, you've had it."

Clark was unimpressed: "No, you run a greater danger of going too fast and burning yourself out so you can't do anything."

We plodded on up the trail, and I occupied my mind by composing letters and my school schedule for the fall semester. We took just under five hours to cover the three and a half miles between Camps II and III, arriving in Camp III more than an hour after Russell's rope. W. Taylor said that they had watched the avalanche from the Hill of Cracks. He repeated what he had said at that time, with his tone of voice indicating growing anxiety: "Hey, that's a big one. Boy, it's getting bigger and bigger. It's heading right for those guys! They're not moving!!"

Taylor asked me if Clark had been slow, and I replied, "He was really draggin'." Taylor said, "He's sure not the ball of fire I used to know."

Wilcox's advance team tried to extend the route from the base of Taylor Spur on 3 July, but heavy new snow had required the re-breaking of the entire trail. They made it only as far as the Flatiron cache, where they dumped their loads.

The Fourth of July dawned beautifully clear and calm. The glacier was decked out with Old Glory colors. Our tents and clothing provided the red, the snow was abundantly white, and the sky a vivid blue. It was an unusual sensation, camping at 8,075 feet on a river of ice, wearing down clothing, all on the Fourth of July. We spent the morning taking pictures, including several group pictures. The early afternoon was mild, and we had ample opportunity to sit outside and shoot the breeze. Luchterhand said, "Next summer I'm going to go someplace warm. No more of this twelve months of winter a year for me." Mosquitoes had been a symbol of the lowlands, and Luchterhand remarked, "Bring on the mosquitoes. I'd be glad to see one now."

A vague rumor had been circulating, to the effect that Wilcox was considering leaving some of the weak climbers behind before we made our summit assault. Schiff and Clark had both been weak and slow, and I wondered if they were the subjects of speculation. I mentioned to Wilcox that, if he was considering leaving some people behind, he would have to make a decision before we left the Muldrow Glacier. Karstens Ridge was too exposed, and the Harper Glacier too high, to leave anyone in camps at those places. Wilcox made no comment about his plans.

Later in the afternoon, I discussed Russell's two-summit-team plan with Janes. Russell had admitted, while at Camp I, that such a plan might cause the second team to lose a chance at good weather for the summit climb. Janes commented on this possibility: "I sure don't intend to spend $300 on this trip and then not make the summit." He was not expressing a "summit at any cost" philosophy, but rather a legitimate concern that his opportunity to reach the top might be impaired by a pre-arranged split in the party.

Wilcox selected the advance team which was to find a route to the crest of Karstens Ridge, and establish Camp V at 12,100 feet on the ridge. Wilcox was in the advance team, along with Russell, W. Taylor, and me. The other eight men were to leave Camp III ahead of us, and push the route from the Flatiron cache on to the head of the Muldrow Glacier. Here they were to establish Camp IV. The advance team would then move up and occupy the camp, while the rest of the group returned to Camp III.

The first two ropes left Camp III in mid-afternoon, and our rope left camp about an hour later, at 16:13. The route rose gently up the lower slopes of the Great Icefall, then crossed a series of deep crevasses to gain the smooth band of glacier between the two sections of the icefall. Off to our left, the icefall was a fantastic array of intersecting crevasses, towering seracs, and crumbling ice. The trail was interesting, with switchbacks among the crevasses, and one spectacular sunken bridge. However, the bridges were all firm, and the icefall was negotiated without great difficulty.

The sun dropped below Pioneer Ridge as we were topping the icefall. We plodded on up the glacier, past the huge, ice-frosted wedge called the "Flatiron." We passed the base of Taylor Spur, and met the other two ropes as they were coming down.

Schlichter said to me, "The next camp is the last one for these boots." We had not yet switched to our high-altitude felt boots. Lewis, Schlichter, and I had all gotten cold feet on this day's climb, because of the slow pace and the intense cold of the snow after the sun had gone down.

I was later told that Schiff had been very slow on the carry to Camp IV. Janes had been setting the downward pace, and he said, "Even with my short legs, Anshel kept saying, 'Go slower. Slow down, the jiggling hurts my stomach.'"

Upon reaching the site selected for Camp IV, we stomped out a tent platform and set up one of the Wilcox group's two orange Logan tents. The camp was located at 11,000 feet, just downglacier from a large crevasse. Luchterhand's team had already probed the tent site for us. We crawled into the tent, and I proceeded to thaw out my very painfully cold feet, while the others started preparing supper. I felt uneasy about the Wilcox group's pyromanic tendencies. I opened my pocket knife and set it on the floor beside me, in case things got too warm in the tent and I had to open a new door in a hurry.

Just my luck—my first meal with the Wilcox group, and this was chili night.

KARSTENS RIDGE
The Tightrope

The Muldrow Glacier is rudely interrupted at an elevation of 11,500 feet by the immense Harper Icefall, which extends upward to 15,000 feet. The icefall is a steep, shattered section of continually avalanching glacier. Avalanches, large and small, rumbled down the Harper Icefall on the average of once every fifteen minutes while we were in Camp IV. The icefall breaks the Muldrow Glacier into two sections, the upper part being called the Harper Glacier. It also makes necessary a detour to the left, up the steep ridge which connects the lower glacier with the upper.

Karstens Ridge is a one-and-a-half-mile-long bridge between the lower reaches of Mount McKinley and the final mass of the peak itself. We gained the crest of the ridge at an elevation below that of Colorado's 11,992-foot Loveland Pass, and left it at an elevation above that of California's 14,495-foot Mount Whitney. Karstens is an exposed, cor-

niced routeway to the summit of Mount McKinley, and it presents the
most challenging technical problem on the Muldrow route.

Karstens Ridge and the upper portion of the peak were cloaked in
heavy fog on the morning of 5 July. We ate a leisurely breakfast, waiting for the clouds to thin so we could see our objective. We left Camp
IV at 12:10, heading directly for the left (east) edge of the glacier and
the base of Karstens Ridge. Wilcox led along the base of the ridge until
we reached 11,300 feet. Here, Russell traded places with Wilcox, and
started breaking trail up the flank of Karstens Ridge.

The route was an ascending traverse, cutting to the left, threading
between the ice cliffs at the base of the ridge and those near its crest.
Fifty yards from the crest of the ridge we switched the rope end for
end, to share in the strenuous task of breaking trail in the hip-deep
snow. Walt Taylor plowed his way to the steep and suspicious wall just
under the crest of the ridge. I held the rope nearly taut, and Taylor
clawed to the top of the ridge. The underlying crevasse, if indeed
there was one, seemed to be solidly bridged. After five hours of hard
slogging from Camp IV, we had reached a saddle on the crest of Karstens Ridge, at an elevation of 11,550 feet.

We dumped our loads at the saddle, and W. Taylor started up the
steep spine of the ridge. The storms of 29 June and 3 July had left a
total of three feet of powder snow on the ridge, and Taylor's thrashing
along the crest with snowshoes was futile and dangerous. The sun was
about to disappear behind Taylor Spur, and we knew the bitter cold of
twilight would soon be upon us. We decided to call it a day, and return tomorrow prepared to force a route through the deep snow to the
proposed campsite at 12,100 feet. Breaking trail uphill with loads from
Camp IV at 11,000 feet to 11,550 feet had taken us five hours. To
cover the same distance unloaded, downhill on a packed trail, took
twenty minutes.

From Karstens we had seen one rope of four men approaching
Camp IV. They had dumped their loads and departed by the time we
reached camp. The second rope arrived later and after a round of hot
punch and tea, returned to Camp III.

After supper, we hauled our down sleeping bags out of their stuff
sacks. W. Taylor shook his vigorously, to give it maximum loft. He en-

couraged it to thicken up by shouting, "Come on you gooses! Fluff up!"

During the night I was troubled by a painfully sunburned face and blistered ears. Due to the light overcast during the day, I had neglected to apply sunburn cream, and the ultraviolet light had taken advantage of its opportunity to roast me. I was careful to apply generous quantities of sunburn cream the next day.

The morning fog dissipated earlier on the sixth than it had the day before, so we left Camp IV just after breakfast. It had snowed only lightly during the night, and the trail was still in good shape. We gained the crest of Karstens Ridge in half the time we had taken the day before, despite a delay that was necessary for snowshoe repairs. Just after leaving Camp IV, Wilcox had broken two snowshoe hinges in two steps.

At the saddle we exchanged our full loads for the lighter loads we had carried the previous day, replaced snowshoes with crampons, and started up the ridge. We ascended the short steep pitch immediately above the saddle, kicking deep steps into the uncertain snow. The steps on this pitch were nearly vertical, some widely spaced, and prone to break out. This first pitch on Karstens provided a stimulating introduction to the ridge.

We had seen two ropes of four working their way up the glacier, and as we topped the first pitch, we saw the leading rope arrive in Camp IV. The second rope was about a mile behind, in the shadow of Taylor Spur. W. Taylor and Russell shouted the phrase that had come to be identified with them, as "Hey mothah!" echoed around the huge amphitheater at the head of the Muldrow Glacier. A reply in kind showed that Luchterhand was in the group at Camp IV.

Wilcox led up the ridge, forcing his way through the three feet of soft snow. We were wearing our crampons for the first time on the mountain, since the ridge was too steep and narrow to allow the use of snowshoes. Wilcox plowed laboriously through the snow, causing small avalanches to cascade down both sides of the ridge. Russell was behind Wilcox, chopping off cornices which were menacing our switchback trail on the ridge flank below. W. Taylor was third, placing wands at fifty-foot intervals, the distance being called off by me as I reached the previously placed wands. Since I was last on the rope, the trail resembled a trench in the ridge crest by the time I reached it. The trench was more than knee deep, and the steps were generally mid-calf deep, affording a very secure feeling.

The clouds enveloped us on the lower part of the ridge and prompted our decision to space the wands closely. This was to prevent anyone from stepping off the ridge and into eternity during a whiteout. The skies alternately cleared and clouded as we progressed up the ridge. We were comfortable in the bright sunshine, and shivering when the sun slipped behind the clouds.

After the first steep pitch the ridge had risen gently, swinging slightly to the left. It was narrow, with steep sides dropping off 500 feet to the Muldrow Glacier on the right and nearly 4,000 feet to the Traleika Glacier on the left, but the gradient of the ridgetop itself was not severe. Our immediate goal was a wide level section of the ridge 550 feet above the saddle where we had first gained the crest. From below, the level section of the ridge appeared as a large hump. Camp V was to be established at the south end of the hump, behind a large detached block of ice, at an elevation of 12,100 feet.

The leftward swing of the ridge ended at the base of the hump, where the ridge turned slightly back to the right. Just as the first pitch on Karstens had been steep, so was the last one before reaching the site of Camp V. To gain the top of the hump, we had to ascend a short steep pitch at its base. The ridge broadened where it joined the base of the hump, dropping off sharply to the left, and sloping gently to the right. Wilcox forced his way up the steep slope. It was steepest, nearly vertical, at the very top of the pitch, and here Wilcox was struggling in soft snow that hit him at chest level. Wilcox topped the pitch and stepped out onto the level crest of the hump. We followed quickly and easily, since a path had been broken through the deep snow. A hundred and fifty easy feet along the level ridge brought us to the site of Camp V, at 12,100 feet. Here we established a cache and looked for possible tent sites.

We returned to the saddle at 11,550 feet, with Wilcox taking the leader's usual descending position at the end of the rope. I set the pace down the ridge, and we fairly flew to the saddle, arriving there in eighteen minutes. We picked up our full loads which we had left at the saddle, and returned to Camp V at 12,100 feet. Breaking the trail from the saddle to Camp V with light loads had taken us three hours and three minutes. We took exactly one-third as much time to go from the saddle to Camp V with full loads, due to the comparative ease of climbing on the broken trail.

The sun hid behind Taylor Spur, and the chill air pressed in on us. We left Camp V and hurried back to Camp IV, arriving there in less than an hour.

Camp III had been struck, leaving only a food cache for the descent, so the entire expedition was now in Camp IV. On the evening of 6 July we had our first radio contact with the rangers at Eielson Visitor Center. We were surprised by the quality of the reception, considering the fact that we were nestled deep in the valley of the Muldrow Glacier, effectively surrounded by mountains on all sides. We strung up a small dipole antenna, which was much more efficient than the vertical antennas built into the radios. Our radios were citizens' band transceivers, one with five watts of power and the other with three.

We had external battery packs for the radios, in addition to the batteries which were in the radios themselves. It was essential to keep the batteries warm to avoid running them down excessively, so the external battery pack was kept inside someone's jacket to be warmed by the body heat. Plug-in wires connected the battery pack to the radio. Wilcox was wearing the battery pack, and he asked Luchterhand, "Do you want to keep the albatross warm for a while?"

"Sure," Luchterhand replied, "gimme the alb."

We chatted for a while, getting acquainted with the radio operators at Eielson. They were Gordon ("Gordie") Haber and George Perkins. Haber inquired about the temperature at our camp. Remembering that Schlichter had worn shorts at Camp II, Luchterhand replied: "It's cold, but you should see these Colorado guys. They're running around in shorts."

Luchterhand was intrigued by Haber's master's thesis study, which involved tracking and observing the habits of wolves in Mount McKinley National Park. Luchterhand expressed a desire to go "wolf chasing" with Haber after our return from the mountain.

Mount McKinley from the east. The sun-tipped ridge at left-center is Karstens Ridge.

Equipment carried on Mount McKinley. Personal gear for one man, plus some Colorado group equipment at lower right. *Photo by James R. Snyder*

Wading the McKinley River. Left to right: Lewis, Russell.

Looking up the Muldrow Glacier to McKinley's North Peak, from McGonagall Pass, the site of Camp I, at 5,720 feet.

Camp II at an elevation of 6,500 feet, in front of the icefalls of Mount Tatum.

Lewis doing his laundry at Camp II.

Lewis peering into the crevasse immediately after being pulled out. *Photo by Mark McLaughlin, courtesy of Jerry M. Lewis*

Mount McKinley from the top of the Lower Icefall, 1 July.

The Fourth of July at Camp III, 8,075 feet. View upglacier toward the shadowed Great Icefall. Karstens Ridge culminates in Browne Tower, the rock outcrop on the left skyline.

The expedition at Camp III. Left to right: S. Taylor, Wilcox, Snyder, Luchterhand, McLaughlin, Schlichter, Clark, Lewis, Schiff, Janes, Russell, W. Taylor.

In the Great Icefall, crossing a fractured bridge across a deep crevasse.
Photo by Jerry M. Lewis

Climbing through the Great Icefall. *Photo by Jerry M. Lewis*

View upglacier from the top of the Great Icefall. Karstens Ridge is on the skyline, with the Harper Icefall at the extreme right.

Karstens Ridge from Camp IV at 11,000 feet. Camp V is at 12,100 feet, in the upper saddle of the ridge.

The Harper Icefall, viewed from Camp IV. The summit of Mount McKinley is obscured by a cloud cap.

Lewis loaded up for a carry to Camp V. Schlichter at right.

Karstens Ridge, viewed from the 11,550-foot saddle. Browne Tower stands at the upper end of the ridge.

At 12,000 feet on Karstens crest.

Camp V at 12,100 feet on Karstens Ridge. Looming beyond the Harper Icefall is an 18,200-foot point on North Peak's Pioneer Ridge.

Karstens Ridge viewed from Camp V at 10:00. Advance team at 12,300 feet.

Haber asked if Mark McLaughlin was in camp with us, because there was a girl at Eielson who had gone to high school with him. McLaughlin took the radio and talked for a while with his former classmate, who was working at the McKinley Park Hotel. She was at Eielson on her day off. An even stranger coincidence was to occur nine days later.

The seventh of July brought with it heavy overcast and light snow. Wilcox selected the advance team which would move up and occupy Camp V, and start pushing the route farther up Karstens Ridge. Luchterhand, McLaughlin, and Clark were selected, but Clark expressed a desire not to be on any advance teams, so Janes took his place. Wilcox was to lead the team once again. The remaining eight of us were to ferry loads from Camp IV to Camp V. Russell spent the morning digging a six-foot-deep, walk-in shelter for the latrine. It was complete with graffiti on the walls.

Wilcox and his group moved up to Camp V in the afternoon. Schlichter, Russell, and the two Taylors went a half mile down the trail to pick up the loads at the Flatiron cache and carry them up to Camp V. Lewis was forced to remain in camp the entire day, as he was stricken with snowblindness. He said it felt like he had hot sand under his eyelids.

I roped up behind Clark, and Schiff tied on behind me. We shouldered our packs and struck off into the heavy fog and light snow. We moved along steadily, and reached Camp V in two hours. When Clark reached the top of the steep pitch just below the camp, he speeded up, moving along easily on the flat ridgetop while Schiff and I were still on the steep section. I stepped up my pace, nearly running up the steep ridge to keep from applying tension to Clark's rope. Schiff yelled, "Slow down!" I adjusted my pace to give Schiff maximum time, while still not slowing Clark down. I did not call for Clark to slow his pace, since we were only 150 feet from Camp V. Once Schiff was safely on the broad, flat ridgetop, he gave a jarring yank on my rope, to express his displeasure with the pace Clark had set.

Upon arrival in Camp V, we unroped and dumped our loads. Wilcox's team had probed the camp and wanded its perimeter, and set up both of the two-man tents. Schlichter's rope arrived in camp soon after we did. I roped up, Schiff and Clark followed suit, and I started to lead down the ridge. I had gotten about fifty feet out of camp when Russell called, "Wait a minute! I want to call a meeting right now! Come back into camp, Howard!"

It seemed like a grandstand trick, to wait until we had already started out of camp to call a meeting. I replied, "Go ahead. I can hear you from here." I stood and waited for the meeting to commence.

Russell said, "Anshel, there's a rumor going around that you have just been carrying half loads." Schiff denied it, and Russell asked what he had carried today. Schiff had carried one Colorado group food bag and the Wilcox group cheese bag, a total of about 44 pounds. This constituted about two-thirds of a normal load.

Clark joined in the fray: "John, I weigh 145 pounds to your 180. I resent the implication that I should be able to carry as much as you."

Russell countered, "I'm willing to carry bigger, heavier loads to help those guys who can't. I just want to know that they're carrying what they're able to." Russell had been claiming that he was carrying the heaviest loads ever since Camp I, while in fact everyone but Clark and Schiff had been carrying tremendous loads, and Clark's were only slightly lighter than anyone else's.

The leadership of the expedition, or the lack of it, was Russell's next target. Turning to Wilcox, he said, "As Fearless Leader, you should be out in the morning, organizing ropes and assigning duties." To Clark he said, "And as Deputy Fearless, you should be doing something too."

Luchterhand retaliated, "No, it's not his job, it's yours and mine. We should all be doing what we can to get things going." Schlichter later told me, "I haven't seen a leader on this climb yet."

The meeting on the high ridge, and in the swirling snow, finally came to an end. We hurried down to Camp IV, leaving Wilcox and his team at Camp V.

When we arrived at Camp IV, W. Taylor made some well-considered remarks, which he had no doubt thought over on the descent: "Anshel, I wasn't going to say anything up there in front of Joe and everyone, but I know you've been carrying half loads ever since McGonagall Pass." Schiff denied this again, and Taylor retorted, "Don't lie Anshel, I know it's true. If you can't carry the loads, that's all right with me, but don't lie about it." He then zeroed in on Clark: "You guys must not have taken Joe's comments seriously about getting in shape for this climb."

Clark said, "I didn't have a lot of time you know, I had to work."

"I don't care about that," Taylor replied. "It doesn't make any sense to be on Mount McKinley and then say you can't do the work and plead physical inability. If it's beyond your physical abilities, you shouldn't be here."

Despite infrequent episodes of frank discussion and criticism, no smoldering resentments were built up. All was soon forgotten, or at least forgiven, in the convivial atmosphere of the chow tent.

The snowstorm of 7 July intensified the next day, and a radio check with Camp V revealed that the wind was whipping Karstens Ridge. Wilcox advised against our moving up from Camp IV to Camp V under these conditions. We spent the day in Camp IV, awaiting a break in the weather.

The storm continued through the morning of 9 July. The clouds parted and the wind died in the afternoon, and we prepared to move up to Camp V. An afternoon radio contact had been scheduled with Wilcox, and W. Taylor asked me to come over to his tent as "a representative of the Colorado group."

I went to W. Taylor's tent, and found S. Taylor and Russell already there. The topic of discussion was Russell's two-summit-team plan. I had hoped that he had given up the idea after our discussion at Mc-Gonagall Pass. I asked what could be the advantage of such an arrangement. Russell contended that the expedition as a whole would have a better chance at the summit if the strongest climbers went first, although he admitted that this would reduce the second team's chances at finding a slot of good weather. He claimed that the plan would aid the second team because they would not have to carry so much food or equipment to the highest camp.

I pointed out that this would be true only if the first team was able to climb immediately from the high camp and then returned to the next lower camp. I said, "I think a summit party of twelve is the best." I knew that circumstances could arise to change the optimum make-up of the summit team, but I did not like the idea of pre-arranging a split for no apparent purpose.

W. Taylor said, "It's not a conspiracy against you personally." I did not see the plan as a conspiracy, only as an unnecessary and potentially disappointing arrangement.

The Wilcox group had left one large food cache at McGonagall Pass, another at Camp III on the Hill of Cracks, and had planned to leave yet another at Camp V on Karstens Ridge. Since the climb from Camp V down to Camp IV was so quick and easy, and carrying loads up the same stretch was fairly difficult, Wilcox had asked me what I thought about leaving the food cache at Camp IV instead of Camp V. I thought it was a good idea. Russell and W. Taylor wanted to move the cache all the way up Karstens to the Harper Glacier, a vertical distance of 4,000 feet. We made our radio contact with Wilcox, and Taylor told Wilcox of his plan for the cache. Taylor asked if we should bring up the so-called "Karstens cache." There was a pause at Wilcox's end of the conversation, and Taylor said, "I told you it'd boggle his mind. Listen to it boggling." Wilcox finally said, "Okay. Bring it up."

After the radio contact, we chatted for a while. Walt Taylor asked Steve Taylor why he had wanted to come on a climb of Mount McKinley. S. Taylor replied, "Oh, to make up for a lot of things in my climbing before this."

W. Taylor was obviously surprised, and he said, "Your climbing couldn't have been that bad."

S. Taylor replied, "Well, it wasn't too good." Walt Taylor and I were astounded. The continent's highest peak is a hazardous place to make up for a lack of previous climbing ability and experience.

The move to Camp V went slowly, due to the wind and snow which had obliterated the packed trail. It was a miserable climb, plagued with numbing cold and a stinging wind gusting around 25 mph. Lewis, by now recovered from his attack of snowblindness, was carrying an extra bulky load, including the Colorado group's cooking utensils. Halfway up the ridge, one of Lewis's crampons became very loose, dangling from its strap. Poor footing, combined with the wind tearing at his oversize load, made Lewis's introduction to Karstens Ridge a far from pleasant, though very memorable occasion.

Upon reaching Camp V, we extended the camp area to accommodate the two Logan tents and the Colorado group's Alp Sport winter expedition tent. We used shovels and snowshoes to dig a wind-breaking trench in which we pitched the tents. Including the snow blocks which we threw up on the edges of the trench, the tents were snuggled down in a hole about six feet deep.

As we had been preparing to leave Camp IV on our way to Camp V, we had seen Wilcox's rope start up the ridge from the upper camp. They returned in the late afternoon, having pushed the route only 200 vertical feet, to the 12,300-foot level. The section of Karstens Ridge above Camp V had two exceptionally steep, narrow pitches. They were both the mountain walls of bergschrunds, with steeply sloping left (southeast) faces, and vertical right (northwest) faces. On the vertical walls we could clearly see the layers of annual snow accumulation. The sharp crests left by these bergschrunds were only slightly corniced, because the prevailing wind was from the west, onto the vertical faces instead of across them. The first bergschrund was at 12,300 feet, the other at 12,700 feet. The advance team had made it to the first bergschrund. The ridge was going to be arduous work.

July tenth arrived calm and clear, the vanguard of four consecutive days of ideal weather. Wilcox dropped out of the advance team, and designated Schlichter to take his place. The advance team started up the ridge at about 09:00. By 13:00 they had reached 12,900 feet and were still going up. At 13:10, Chief Park Ranger Arthur J. Hayes and glacier pilot Don Sheldon buzzed our camp and the climbers on Karstens Ridge. We waved and took pictures of the plane as it zoomed by. Our climb was proceeding according to plan; all was well.

The advance team reached 13,200 feet, having started up the broad, steep slope at the base of the Coxcomb, the steepest portion of Karstens Ridge. Here they encountered a section of steep wind slab, and decided to push no further. They had done a full day's work, breaking trail from 12,300 feet to 13,200 feet, and installing pickets and securing fixed line over the crest of the bergschrund at 12,700 feet. They descended, pausing to establish a cache at the base of the Coxcomb at 13,000 feet, and then moved on down the ridge to camp.

Lewis and I had spent the morning fitting our adjustable crampons to our high-altitude felt boots. We had decided to climb the ridge at night, when the snow would be frozen for easier and drier climbing. The evening sun skittered along the crest of Pioneer Ridge, a fiery ball rolling down the mountain slope. The cold became intense without the tempering influence of the direct sunlight, and I broke out my expedition down parka, pants, and mitts for the first time.

We packed our loads and prepared to start up the ridge at about 17:00. Wilcox was leading the first rope, with S. Taylor, Schiff, and Clark, in that order. Our rope was composed of Russell, myself, Lewis, and W. Taylor, in order. We started up the trail about ten minutes after Wilcox had left camp. Our rope had gotten about fifty feet out of camp when the sliding bar which adjusted the length of one of my crampons pulled out, breaking the crampon in two. I stopped to check the crampon, and determined that it would take some time to repair, so we turned around and started back to camp.

We had taken less than half a dozen steps when one of Lewis's crampons likewise pulled apart. We spent about an hour in camp, working on the crampons. I bent the ends of the metal bars to keep them from sliding out of position, while Lewis preferred to tie the crampon sections together with alpine cord, thus eliminating the bars and the chain links which joined the heel and toe sections of the crampons.

Our repairs were finished at about 18:00, and we started out again, an hour behind Wilcox's rope. We found the fixed line installed by the advance team at 12,600 feet. We clipped into the fixed line with carabiners and slings, and moved cautiously up the steep, broad ridge. The ridge narrowed to a crest, arcing to the right and going over the crest of the second bergschrund wall. The fixed line ran from 12,600 feet to 12,700 feet, ending where the bergschrund faded into the temporarily broad and gentle ridgetop. We hurriedly crossed the crest of the bergschrund, because from below it could not be determined whether or not it was corniced.

Once we had topped the bergschrund, we could see Wilcox's rope ahead of us, moving very slowly. They sat down in the snow at 12,900 feet, just below the Coxcomb cache. We caught up with them despite their one-hour head start from Camp V. Wilcox's rope had already been sitting for ten minutes when we caught up with them, and Russell decided we would sit and wait also, rather than pass them up. Their rope had switched end-for-end, so that Clark was now in the lead. Wilcox and Clark were the picture of exhaustion, sitting with the snow blowing over them, their shoulders sagging and their heads bowed.

I was wearing my down parka and pants, which were much too warm while we were moving at a consistent pace up the ridge, but which were very comfy while sitting immobile in the stinging wind. W. Taylor was more moderately dressed, and cold gave rise to well-founded impatience. "What're they doing up there?!" Taylor shouted. Russell replied that they were just sitting, doing nothing. We sat for about fifteen minutes, and then Taylor could take no more: "John, tell 'em to move up to the cache! Let's get going!"

Haltingly, and with loud complaints from Clark and Schiff, they started moving up to the cache, less than 100 yards away. One wonders, had they intended to sit there forever? Clark finally abandoned his pack beside the trail and continued on to the cache. We all gathered at the cache, which was behind the smaller of the only two rocks which are found on Karstens crest. Wilcox, Schiff, and Clark had had enough; they and S. Taylor would return to Camp V. Our rope decided to go on, to finish the route up Karstens Ridge if we could.

We moved quickly up the broad, steep slope of the Coxcomb, using the bucket steps left by the advance team. At 13,200 feet the steps ran out, where the advance team had turned back after encountering steep, hard, wind-slab snow. We cramponed up the slab, teetering precariously on our oversized boots. I was trying a footgear combination of my own invention, including the use of down booties inside my felt boots (Wilcox had also thought of using down booties). My boots were wonderfully warm, but lacking in control on steep cramponing pitches.

The wind slab lasted for only about fifty feet, and then we were wallowing in deep snow. Russell was leading, hacking his way through deep sastrugi ruts by holding his ice ax horizontally with one end in each hand, and pulling the soft snow down in huge blocks. I followed, kicking steps into the trough left by Russell. We angled generally toward the right edge of the broad ridge, which became narrower and narrower as we approached the top of the Coxcomb. It was now 01:00 on 11 July, and the rising sun was turning North Peak a burnished gold. Off to our left, the 10,335-foot-high Mooses Tooth squatted in blue darkness at McKinley's feet. To our right, we peered down on the jumbled mass of the Harper Icefall, and straight ahead loomed golden-hued Browne Tower.

At 02:30, we reached 14,500 feet, and gazed up the Harper Glacier, a sunrise-gilded carpet rolling gently toward the summit. We had entered the realm of the high mountain for the first time, and I looked with awe upon the frozen, silent, dawn-tinted world that awaited us. Under these conditions of perfect weather and fantastic lighting, it was easy to see why Archdeacon Hudson Stuck had likened the Harper basin to "the hall of the mountain king."

Russell was understandably worn out from breaking trail up 1,300 feet of the ridge, and wanted to start back for camp. I felt strongly compelled to push on, because for the first time since starting up Karstens Ridge we could see our goal, the South Peak of Mount McKinley, glowing in the sunrise. I could identify Denali Pass and Archdeacons Tower, and the summit looked as though we could reach out and touch it—when in reality it was still 6,000 vertical feet above us. I wanted to go at least as far as Parker Pass, marked by an outcrop of rocks at 14,600 feet, about 200 yards ahead of us. The so-called "pass" is actually the point where the route leaves Karstens Ridge and begins its traverse across the flank of Browne Tower and onto the Harper Glacier. Lewis was willing but not eager to push on, and Russell and Taylor were against it, so we dumped our loads at 14,500 feet.

We had put in a long, hard day. We had been climbing for eight and a half hours, and had forced the route up Karstens Ridge to a point where it blends into the slope of Browne Tower. To complete a route up Karstens Ridge had required four separate advance teams and five climbing days, but now it was done. The road to the summit was clear.

The sun was brilliant and hot as we approached Camp V at 12,100 feet, and we sweltered in our high-altitude clothing. The descent to camp required only one hour and twenty minutes, even though we had taken time to install fixed line from 13,300 feet on the Coxcomb down to the cache at 13,000 feet.

Schlichter, Luchterhand, McLaughlin, and Janes left Camp V around 11:00 on the eleventh, to extend the route across the west face of Browne Tower and onto the Harper Glacier. They were to select a site for Camp VI, hopefully around 15,200 feet. The remaining eight of us were to move our personal gear and camp supplies up to the Harper Glacier and establish Camp VI. We were to leave Camp V in the evening, giving the advance team plenty of time to break the trail onto the Harper and select a campsite.

Lewis and I spent the afternoon packing our gear and reinforcing the quick crampon repairs we had made the previous day. The sun went behind Pioneer Ridge, and Karstens Ridge slowly succumbed to shadow. As the sun slipped farther down Pioneer Ridge it made a comeback attempt, shining through low gaps in the ridge. After four hours of shade, our camp was bathed in rosy-hued light at 22:00. The sun sank lower and centered itself in a gap on Pioneer Ridge, spreading its pink glow up the northwest face of Karstens Ridge and illuminating the very top of Browne Tower so that it looked like a lighthouse.

We formed the same rope teams as we had the day before, and Wilcox's rope departed Camp V around 21:00. Our rope left camp at 23:15, thus giving Wilcox more than a two-hour head start. We wanted to avoid a repetition of the previous night's experience, since we did not enjoy sitting like sled dogs in the blowing snow.

As we approached the Coxcomb cache, we saw the advance team starting down the steep slope of the Coxcomb. We reached the cache, and waited a couple of minutes for the advance team to arrive. Janes was the first man down, and I asked him where they had located the camp. He said it was on the near (southeast) side of the glacier, at the end of the traverse across the slopes of Browne Tower. The men had gotten their first view of the South Peak, Archdeacons Tower, and Denali Pass, and they were enthusiastic about pushing on for the summit.

I told Luchterhand of my calculations regarding our day of arrival at the summit. I said that we should make the summit on 16 July, to which Luchterhand replied, "And then the storm hits that knocks the hell out of us."

The advance team descended to Camp V, and we continued on up the ridge. It was now 01:00 on 12 July, and the rising sun in the northeast set the sky aflame, causing the hundreds of kettle lakes near the McKinley River to shine like beacons. The river itself was a twisting band of sparkling silver. Wonder Lake, our idea of civilization, shone like a large city. The maze of crevasses on the Muldrow Glacier sulked in the shadows, dark and menacing. We wondered how we had threaded our way through them.

The gently ascending traverse across the side of Browne Tower was negotiated with care, because of the breakaway nature of the loose snow overlying iron-hard windcrust. A slip here could have ended in one of the numerous crevasses on the Harper Glacier at the base of the slope. Leading our rope, Walt Taylor reached the high point of the traverse, about 150 yards out of Camp VI. He turned toward the three of us who were still delicately poised on the traverse and said, "I'm on top, gentlemen. It's all downhill from here."

We arrived in Camp VI just as the sun was reaching the broiling point. We had been on the trail five hours and three minutes from Camp V. Karstens Ridge was below us now. Above us, the Harper Glacier rose toward Denali Pass, a giant staircase with icefalls for steps.

⌐⌐⌐⌐⌐⌐⌐ **6** ⌐⌐⌐⌐⌐⌐⌐

THE HARPER GLACIER
In the Hall
of the Mountain King

Camp VI was located at 15,000 feet on the Harper Glacier, at the northeast corner of a level stretch above the Harper Icefall. The camp was bordered by the slopes of Browne Tower and the top of the Harper Icefall. The first crevasse of the icefall was only forty feet downglacier from camp. Above the camp, the Harper Glacier was bounded on the right by the ice slopes and rock buttresses of North Peak, while on the left lay the completely glacier covered slopes of the South Peak. Our route was to follow the Harper to 18,200-foot Denali Pass, then continue up the ridge from the pass to the south summit.

The twelfth of July was a scorcher at 15,000 feet, too hot for comfortable sleeping in the tents. The air temperature was in the low twenties, but the sensible temperature was pleasant enough to allow us to walk around in our shirtsleeves, thanks to the intense sunlight. For the first time on our climb there was literally not a cloud in the sky, not even as far as we could see in any direction toward the horizon.

In the afternoon, Wilcox and I built latrine shelters into the slope

88

beside camp. For some reason, Wilcox wanted two latrines. I dug one shelter, of simple design and solid construction, while Wilcox built another. He labored to produce a monument to civilization, which he equipped with a mirror, a paper flower, and a bottle of hand lotion. Clark studied the two constructions for a moment, then set to work with a roll of adhesive tape and two snowshoes. Before long he had made letters from the tape and attached them to the mesh of the snowshoes. Clark placed a snowshoe on the trail in front of each privy, clearly designating the plain one for "MEN," the other for "WOMEN."

Just before supper, I was outside the tent gathering pans full of snow to be melted down. Walt Taylor and Russell had dug a hole in the snow wall beside their tent, to serve as a refrigerator for their evening Jello. Since I was outside, they handed me their bowl of Jello and asked me to put it in their refrigerator. I complied, and then crawled into our tent to start cooking supper. Taylor and Russell had pitched their Logan tent with its front door facing the front door of our Colorado group tent. We placed a ski pole between the two tents, so that both tents could use it as an anchor point for their front guy lines.

In sunny, calm weather the Colorado group cooked its meals outside, while under cold or snowy conditions we cooked in the tent. Whenever wind conditions allowed, we tied the front tunnel entrance open while cooking in the tent, to prevent the buildup of noxious stove fumes. The tent door was open on this cold, calm night, and we could hear W. Taylor and Russell in their tent, pumping up a stove to start cooking their supper. Suddenly, Lewis and I heard a loud "whump!" and looked out the front door to see a flaming stove hurtling directly toward us, having been pitched out of Taylor and Russell's tent. Just in front of our open door, the stove hit an ice bump, and slid off our tent platform, coming to a stop on the trail which ran through the center of the camp.

Down at 12,100 feet, the men in Camp V spent the warm midday hours resting up for the night's work. Wilcox's pre-expedition correspondence came up as a topic of discussion. He had sent newspaper clippings to each of the members of his group and to me, clippings concerned with Wilcox's climbing activities. Luchterhand said that

Wilcox was leading the expedition because, "He wants to be known as a great mountaineer."

Aside from Wilcox, none of the men in his group shared his ideas about publicity. They found the name of the expedition quite humorous, and had long been referring to it as the "Wilcox Memorial Expedition." McLaughlin envisioned a second, third, fourth, etc., annual Wilcox Memorial Expedition.

On the evening of 12 July, Luchterhand, Janes, McLaughlin, and Schlichter broke Camp V at 12,100 feet, and prepared to move up to Camp VI. After packing their loads, they cached some equipment for a later carry and collected the trash around the campsite. A one-liter plastic fuel bottle had developed a leak, so one liter of precious white gas was used to fuel the trash fire. As before at Camp II, odds and ends of food were burned rather than cached. The spare radio batteries were buried, to be retrieved on the descent. No one in the Colorado group was consulted or informed about this action. We were now without any spare batteries for the remainder of the ascent.

The four men from Camp V arrived in Camp VI at 01:00 on 13 July. I had been watching the four-hour continuous process of sunset and sunrise at 15,000 feet, a spectacle never to be forgotten. As the rope from 12,100 feet arrived in camp, the solar display was especially intense, and six shutterbugs proceeded to record the event. A bright shaft of light pierced the orange-red clouds on the horizon, rising like a searchlight beam from the appearing sun. This was Mount McKinley at its kindest and most beautiful.

The thirteenth of July proved to be our fourth clear, calm day in a row. The team which had just arrived in Camp VI had no specific task to accomplish, other than to catch up on their eating and sleeping. Wilcox assigned Lewis, Russell, W. Taylor, and me to bring up the last loads from Camp V. Wilcox, Schiff, Clark, and S. Taylor were to find and mark the route up the Harper toward Denali Pass.

S. Taylor had been feeling the effects of altitude ever since the 12,100-foot camp, though he kept the fact that he was ill pretty much to himself. I asked him if he would prefer to trade places with me, and go with the team to Camp V and back. He agreed, thinking the lower altitude might be beneficial. I wanted to accompany the advance team because my large boots were massaging my toes to numbness, due to the extreme flexing of the boots while being used on the steep sections of Karstens Ridge. Besides, I was eager to explore the upper reaches of the Harper Glacier. The summit was in constant view, a longtime goal now within reach, providing continuous stimulation.

The advance team descended to 14,500 feet to bring up the food that had been cached there two days before. Lewis, Russell, and the Taylors accompanied us to the Browne Tower cache, and then continued on down Karstens Ridge toward Camp V, to pick up the last loads there. The advance team packed the goods from the cache, and returned to Camp VI.

In Camp VI we modified our loads for a carry upglacier, taking food bags that were intended for use several days later. Luchterhand was trying to cook breakfast on one of the Wilcox group's balky stoves, which had been bashed and abused ever since Camp I. All four of the stoves were giving trouble in varying degrees, a consequence of continual overpriming, overpumping, and rough handling. Russell had been "repairing" the stoves because, he said, the gaskets were no good. He had been using the bottoms of cardboard salt shakers as replacement gaskets. Schiff, who had shown an early and continuing concern for the abuse of equipment on the climb, said "Russell is ruining these stoves, and now he wants to work on it again." Schiff suggested that the cardboard gasket be replaced with some leather from the repair kit. Luchterhand advised, "Work on it before he [Russell] gets back."

Wilcox borrowed Luchterhand's Alaskan trail snowshoes, to break trail above Camp VI, and we left camp at 13:46, heading diagonally up and across the gentle glacier so as to skirt the Harper Glacier's central icefall on its right (north) side. Wilcox carried a ten-foot bamboo pole, with which he probed the route for crevasses.

At 15,600 feet, we started up the slope leading to the side of the central icefall, and the use of snowshoes became difficult in the steep, loose snow. By the time we reached 15,900 feet, Wilcox needed a rest, so Clark took the lead position on the rope. Clark put on the trail snowshoes, while Schiff and I doffed our snowshoes in favor of crampons. In less than a rope length, we topped the steep snowslope, and cut sharply to the left, heading directly upglacier beside the icefall.

The going was easy, because the loose snow cover had decreased to only about four inches, and the terrain was gentle. We were cautious though, because numerous bumps and sags indicated the presence of crevasses. One such bump was composed of blue ice, the first solid, non-granular ice we had seen on the climb. At 16,400 feet, we surmounted the central Harper icefall, and skirted around its top and out onto the nearly level stretch of glacier that lay above.

The terrain became increasingly easy, with shallow snow cover and no sign of crevasses. A pale half moon hung in the windless sky just over McKinley's summit. By 18:50 we had reached 16,500 feet, and Clark called a halt. Clark and Schiff wanted to dump their loads and return to Camp VI. But our light advance-team loads, perfect weather, and the nearness of Denali Pass tempted me to keep going upward. I suggested to Wilcox that he and I go on and select the site for Camp VII near Denali Pass, while the others returned to Camp VI. Almost wordlessly, he declined.

We cached our loads, including Luchterhand's snowshoes, and started back for Camp VI. As we descended the slope beside the central icefall, we could see four minute black specks on the wall of snow below Browne Tower. They were Lewis, Russell, and the Taylors returning to Camp VI with the last equipment loads from Camp V. Also visible downglacier were clouds, lapping at McKinley's feet. They were the first clouds we had seen in three days.

Our pace across the flat snow above Camp VI was quite slow, and I took the opportunity to mash down the walls between our footprints, thus making a continuous level trench out of what had been a series of post holes.

Upon arrival at Camp VI, Wilcox, Clark, and Schiff disappeared into one of their group's Logan tents, and I crawled into the Colorado group tent. Schlichter and Lewis had a hot steak dinner waiting for me, which I enjoyed all the more due to a hard day's work, the magnificent surroundings, and most of all, good companions.

As we ate, I mentioned that Wilcox had been slow today, and had not wanted to go on toward Denali Pass. Later, in Camp VII, McLaughlin told me that Wilcox had been affected by the altitude ever since reaching Camp VI, at 15,000 feet, and probably on Karstens Ridge as well. Had it not been for Wilcox's illness, ensuing events might have been different.

The entire Wilcox group gathered for supper, and the Colorado group could tell that a meeting was in progress, although we could not hear just what was being said. After the nightly 20:00 radio contact with Eielson Visitor Center, Wilcox walked over to our tent.

"We're going to have two summit teams," he informed us, "the first one with eight and the second one with four."

"And?" I asked.

"And you'll be in the first team."

"Jerry and Paul too?"

"Yes, you're all in the first group. Walt and John are in the second team, and Steve and Anshel have asked to be in the second team so they could stay here for a day. They're not feeling too good."

So Russell's plan for two summit teams had won out. The second team was composed of W. Taylor, Russell, S. Taylor, and Schiff, four of the least experienced men in the expedition.

Wilcox continued: "Eielson says there's a storm coming in on the sixteenth. We'll go up [to Camp VII] tomorrow, and Saturday [15 July] will be our summit day. The second team will move up to the high camp on Saturday. We're going to combine all food and kitchen gear from here on up. We'll use our food and stoves, and you can cache your stuff here."

"When the second team comes up," I said, "that'll mean splitting ten men's food twelve ways." [3]

"There's enough to be able to stretch it," Wilcox assured me. "John will select all the equipment and arrange it into loads. We want to get an early start tomorrow."

Wilcox left, and we mulled over the prospects. I had mixed feelings. I was eager to start for the summit, and was excited now that we were ready to begin the summit assault. There had been some talk of establishing an intermediate camp somewhere around 16,500 to 17,000 feet,

[3] Though only nine in number, the Wilcox group was carrying pre-packaged food for ten men.

and I was glad that this plan had been scrapped. I still could see no reason for the split party, and I was a bit apprehensive about depending on the Wilcox group's food and stoves, since both left a great deal to be desired. But it was only for a couple or three days, so we figured we could make do with the Wilcox group's bill of fare for a while. To have insisted on taking our own food and stoves would have caused too much friction, so we had just quietly agreed to the use of Wilcox's gear. The purpose, of course, was to provide three more pack animals for the same amount of gear, thus allowing lighter loads.

Sleep was most difficult that night, and I was up at 04:00, cooking breakfast outside in the bright sunshine. I noted in my logbook, "Some clouds appearing very early in lowlands." Our perfect weather was changing, and the clouds were moving slowly up the mountain toward us. We ate a filling breakfast of tea, hot cereal, orange juice, and scrambled eggs with ham, then finished off the last of our bacon.

At 07:30, the Colorado group was in its tent sorting gear, selecting only those items that we needed for the high camp and the summit climb. Wilcox, Luchterhand, Janes, S. Taylor, Russell, and W. Taylor were in the Logan tent which was facing our tent, finishing a late breakfast. We heard the all-too-familiar "whump!" of an exploding stove, and expected to see the stove come flying out the door as it had the night before last. But instead we saw the Logan tent burst into a ball of flame, and heard the mad scrambling of people trying to get out of the burning tent. Someone kicked a pot full of cocoa, and it crashed down on top of our tent, showering hot cocoa through the fabric of the tent and over our gear inside. Schlichter dove out the front door of our tent, Lewis squirmed through the back door, while I stayed put. I had the foolish notion that if our tent caught fire, I would try to put it out by pulling it down from the inside.

The fire had lasted three seconds, all the time it took to completely disintegrate the Logan tent. The men in the tent had been using two stoves simultaneously, a hazardous practice at best. One had almost burned dry, and W. Taylor decided to refill it. Instead of taking the stove outside, he opened the filler cap while the stove was sitting right beside the still-burning second stove. As the cap was unscrewed, the pressurized fumes from the fuel tank filled the tent, and were immediately ignited by the second stove. Taylor was crouched over the stoves, and when the explosion occurred he dived forward against the side wall of the tent. By the time he got there the wall was gone, and he fell out onto the snow. The tent disappeared as though it had evaporated, leaving only the zippers and the neoprene coated floor.

I crawled out of our tent to survey the wreckage. Boots, caps, pots, and pans were spread out randomly in the snow around the tent floor, and in the middle of the floor sat one of the stoves, still sputtering with small flames. Russell glared at the stove, then gave it a hard kick, sending it flying past the remaining Logan tent, spewing burning gasoline as it sailed by. Several men immediately pounced on the burning tent, beating out the flames before any damage was done.

As things quieted down a bit, we started counting our losses, and found that we had been quite lucky. W. Taylor had sustained minor burns on his left hand, as well as singed hair and eyebrows. Janes had been kicked in the forehead during the scramble to escape the tent. He had a small cut, but was otherwise unharmed. Materiel losses, in addition to the tent, were W. Taylor's down jacket and Russell's down sleeping bag. Schiff had a double down jacket, and he gave one jacket to Taylor, while McLaughlin split his double sleeping bag with Russell.

The Wilcox group had been using special waterproof matches on the expedition. Over the past weeks, the matches had proved to be not only waterproof, but nearly fireproof as well. A bundle of matches sat triumphantly in the middle of the tent floor. Russell looked at them, and saw a bright spot in our situation: "There's one thing that didn't burn—the company matches."

"Everyone was feeling so good," Schlichter said to me, "and then this happened." The fire had shaken us, and tumbled our high "summit day" spirits. Before we had completely cleaned up the mess left by the fire, the clouds seeped up the glacier and quietly engulfed us. Working now in the fog, we finished packing our summit gear and cached everything else on our tent platform, covering the cache with Schlichter's poncho. To avoid sending the five-gallon gasoline can to the high camp, Russell borrowed the Colorado group's one-gallon can, emptying the kerosene it contained into a Wilcox group honey jar. Although the honey was in small plastic packets rather than loose in the jar, I nonetheless hoped we would not have to use the kerosene from that jar.

At 11:00, Wilcox's rope with McLaughlin, Luchterhand, and Janes started up the trail and disappeared into the fog. Lewis, Schlichter, and Clark were on my rope, and we took the last of the high camp loads that had been made up by Russell. The four men who were remaining at Camp VI were going to use Colorado group food this night, so I wished W. Taylor a happy pork chop dinner. Taylor said he was really looking forward to a good dinner, a welcome change from the Wilcox group's food. By 11:20, we had finished our chores at the 15,000-foot camp, and started up the glacier toward Denali Pass. I waved my ice ax to the men in Camp VI. "See ya tomorrow!"

We had gone about a half mile when Clark said he smelled gasoline fumes. He took off his pack, and gave his one-gallon fuel can an intensive inspection. After tightening the lid and securing the can in his pack, Clark spent a few more minutes adjusting his pack. Finally, after sighting through a 360-degree panorama with his camera without taking a single picture, Clark was ready to go. Another half mile was ground off, and just as we were approaching the base of the central Harper icefall, my left crampon broke in two. Another delay was required. The chain link joining the front and back halves of the crampon had snapped. Lewis had replaced his chain links with nylon cord, and he gave me his old chain, which was soon installed and we were on our way again.

The sun had begun to break through the clouds while we were stopped for crampon repairs, and as we ascended the edge of the central icefall, the sun burned off the clouds, raising our hopes for good summit weather the next day. At 16,400 feet, where the trail rounded the top corner of the icefall and started back out onto the glacier, we caught up with Wilcox's rope. All four men were sitting in the snow, presumably enjoying the bright sunshine and calm air. Clark asked the men on Wilcox's rope, "Do any of you want to get on this express train?" Luchterhand replied, "No, I'll just stick with the slow freight."

We stood on the trail for about five minutes, then I asked Janes how long they had been sitting there. "I don't know," he replied, "but too long. About twenty minutes."

We waited another ten minutes, and then two delta wing jets roared overhead. Air Force Lieutenant Schlichter commented: "That's the way I'll come up here next time. Those guys are looking down here and saying, 'Look at those idiots!' "

By now my rope had been stopped for nearly twenty minutes, and I was getting tired of waiting, so I said, "Joe, how about us going on and breaking trail?" Wilcox readily agreed, and we took the lead. We started moving upglacier, and Clark called out to everyone in general and someone in particular, "He'll slow down when we reach the cache and he has to start breaking trail."

We stopped at the 16,500-foot cache only long enough to pick up the probe pole. The food was to be left there, because, said Wilcox, "We could always come down from the high camp and get it if we need more food."

At 16,800 feet, near the base of the upper Harper icefall, we encountered a small but persistent crevasse. Unable to find a bridge over the crevasse, or make an end run around it, we finally decided to jump it. Then we started up the last relatively steep slope on the Harper Glacier, that beside the upper icefall. The soft snow here was eight to twelve inches deep, the most we had found this day. The clouds closed in again, and our world of sparkling white, blue, and gold took on a somber gray hue. I slogged along breaking trail, and finally established a thirty-steps-then-rest routine. Clark, at the end of the rope where the trail had already been broken by three men, started calling out, "Slower, slower!"

We topped the icefall at 17,400 feet, and headed straight up the gently sloping glacier toward Denali Pass, which lay one mile ahead and 800 feet higher. "About a mile a week slower!" Clark called out.

Schlichter asked when we would be making camp, and I said about seven (19:00). "Let's agree on seven for the time to stop and set up camp," Schlichter said. I agreed, thinking we would be to Denali Pass by that time. But the pass was farther than it seemed.

Around ten minutes to 19:00, Schlichter said it was about time to stop. I glanced at my watch, then looked upglacier. I said that we should make it to the pass at about seven-thirty (19:30). Schlichter calmly replied, "We agreed on seven. You could keep moving it back all night. Let's stop at seven."

Time was limited now, and I may have unconsciously stepped up the pace. As we neared 17,900 feet, Clark cut loose with both barrels: "Damn it, slow down! I can go all the way to the summit *today* if you want to, if we just go slow!"

"Well, Jerry," I replied, "I guess when people start cussing me out, it's time to stop." Clark seemed a little embarrassed by his uncharacteristic outburst, and he explained that he thought it was about time to make camp. I agreed, but insisted that we move upglacier a couple hundred feet and establish camp near the foot of the uppermost granite buttress of North Peak. This rock buttress was free of snow, and thus we would not be subject to the avalanche hazard posed by the snow faces further downglacier. We moved up to 17,900 feet, and here we established Camp VII. I had hoped to put Camp VII at 18,200 feet, in the lee of the ridge that runs from Denali Pass to the South Peak, but my hopes were not to be realized.

We dumped our loads and fell to clearing tent platforms. A light breeze had started blowing, and it was to increase through the night. As expected, this was the coldest camp yet. The temperature was less than ten degrees, and falling. Wilcox's rope dragged slowly up the glacier, and we wondered what could be wrong. They arrived in camp, and we found out that Luchterhand was very ill. A tent was hurriedly set up for Luchterhand, and he crawled into his sleeping bag, unable to eat any dinner.

Supper that night included pea soup. The Colorado group liked pea soup, and we had it in our own meals. But in our menus it was merely billed as soup; in the Wilcox group's meal it was the main course. So with a hearty bowl of pea soup, we were fortified for the summit climb on the morrow.

THE SUMMIT

Wind raked our camp all night, rattling the tents and burying the equipment which was left outside. On the morning of 15 July, I peered anxiously out the front door of our tent. The view was not encouraging. Snow and clouds, driven by a 25- to 30-mph wind, made it impossible to see even across the Harper Glacier, a distance of a half mile. I busied myself with transferring my gear from my Kelty expedition pack to my small Gerry summit pack, looking out the door periodically to check on the weather. Around 10:00, the snow stopped falling and the clouds began to disperse. We could see the slopes across the Harper Glacier, dimly at first, but growing more distinct with the passing minutes. A look upglacier revealed the lowest rocks on the ridge near Denali Pass.

The long-awaited moment seemed imminent: it was time to make ready for the summit climb. From inside our tent, I called to Wilcox's tent, "Joe, are you guys about ready to go?"

"Are you guys getting anxious?" came Wilcox's reply.

"You're darn right we're anxious," I said. Here we were at our high camp, with a possible slot of good weather coming up. The rangers had warned us by radio on the night of 13 July that today would be our last day of good weather for a time, with a storm due to move in tomorrow, 16 July. It is essential to both safety and success on Mount McKinley that a good day never be wasted, especially high on the mountain. Washburn had made this point more than once in his writings on Mount McKinley.

We were likely to encounter high-velocity winds and extremely low temperatures during the summit climb. These hazards were accentuated by the altitude and the exposed nature of the route. We would be completely open to the full force of the west wind. Up to now, the wind had always been moderated somewhat by the valley walls beside us and the bulk of Mount McKinley to the west of us. Once we reached Denali Pass and started up the ridge toward the summit, however, we would be climbing on McKinley's leading edge, the ridge that slices the onrushing frozen air.

With these things in mind, Schlichter, Lewis, and I prepared for the climb. Over our usual net underwear, shirts, and ski pants, we donned down shirts, down pants, and windbreaker shell parkas. Down parkas were stuffed into our packs, along with lunch, emergency signaling equipment, spare socks and mitts, flags, and a map. Our feet were of special concern, and we prepared for the coldest conditions. A pair of silk socks was put on first, followed by a pair of heavy woollen socks, then down booties, felt boots, felt overboot insulation, and nylon overboots. We pulled our down mittens on over thick silk gloves, and crawled out of the tent at 11:30.

Wilcox was nearly ready to go, but the other four were still in their tents. I found it hard to believe that they didn't want to go on to the summit today, since by now the sky was a bright blue and the wind had dropped to about 5 mph. I walked over to Clark's tent. "Jerry, are any of you guys goin' up today?"

Clark answered for all of them, "I think we'll just sit and watch the snow blow." A few minutes later, Clark said that maybe he and McLaughlin would climb North Peak today. I asked if they wanted to go as far as Denali Pass with us, since Washburn's North Peak route starts about there. Clark declined, saying they would climb directly from Camp VII, ascending a couloir just downglacier from camp.

Starting at Camp I, we had climbed the mountain with a consistent pattern: an advance team of four and a follow-up group of eight. But the plan devised on 13 July, while we were at Camp VI, had called for the first summit team to include eight men. Whether by chance or design, we were once again using an advance team of four, just as we had always done before. We searched the camp for wands to mark the route, and found that Russell had kept most of them in Camp VI. We had fewer than thirty wands to mark the two-mile route to the summit.

We lashed our crampons onto our boots, and I tied a spare ice ax onto my pack. We roped up, and with a shout of "Hi-ho!" we were on our way to the summit.

We placed wands every rope length, breaking our four-foot wands in half and sticking them only six inches into the snow. The half mile to Denali Pass was nearly level, but the going was difficult due to a weak wind crust which would hold me up momentarily, then break through as my full weight was placed on my forward foot. The soft snow started to thin out as we neared Denali Pass, and we encountered more wind-blasted slabs of hard snow. We had left Camp VII at 12:03, and at 12:50 we reached Denali Pass, at an elevation of 18,200 feet. Here we found a large cache of wooden crates. We did not know what was inside, but we could see that the crates had been broken open. We presumed it was Washburn's cache of food and equipment, and thought that the Winter McKinley Expedition had probably broken into it the previous February.

We spent a few minutes at the pass, excited by our first view of Mount Foraker, McKinley's 17,400-foot companion to the southwest. From the slopes of The Great One, we gazed at Mount Foraker, The Great One's wife. The wind on the pass was a mere breeze; above us drifted serene altostratus clouds, while cottony cumulus clouds lapped at the hills 10,000 feet below us.

At 13:13 we started up the ridge toward South Peak, and to our delight we found the ridge to be composed of very hard, wind-packed snow. The ridge was perfect for cramponing, requiring neither the kicking nor the cutting of steps. We stopped for a radio contact at the 18,400-foot level of the ridge. Wilcox called Eielson and arranged for a radio check every two hours during our summit climb. Schlichter wanted to fire a smoke bomb on the summit, so we asked permission from the Park Service. Eielson said that they would check with head-quarters, and let us know. Wilcox informed Eielson that another climbing party of two might be attempting North Peak today. We could see Camp VII and the entire North Peak route from our vantage point. However, no one was stirring anywhere around the camp, so it seemed unlikely that Clark and McLaughlin would try North Peak today. Wilcox signed off, and we continued up the ridge.

The weather, which had been good ever since noon, got even better. The altostratus clouds gave way to high, scattered cirrus clouds in a splendid dark blue sky. At some anonymous point on the ridge, we passed the 18,619-foot level, and with it we passed Schlichter's and my previous high-altitude mark.

There was no wind. Although the world seemed to hold its breath, we did not hold ours. Lewis, just behind me on the rope, was breathing heavily. I could hear Wilcox at the end of the rope, puffing like a steam locomotive. Lewis started to feel the effects of the altitude, and began calling for short rest stops. As soon as we would stop, Lewis would sprawl out on the hard snow, and Wilcox would sit down. After four or five minutes, I would say, "Ready, Jerry?" and Lewis would be up and climbing again.

At 19,100 feet on the ridge, we encountered the first cornice, a bee-tling brow of snow which hung in trackless space overlooking the Ka-hiltna Glacier. Some weather was starting to develop now, and from where we stood we could see it coming. No surprise storms should catch us up here, because every cloud was presented as though for our inspection. Stratus clouds were beginning to spread along the glaciers to the west, while on the southwestern horizon large cumulonimbus clouds were raising their anvil-shaped heads. Directly above us the sky remained clear, and the air calm.

We had nearly finished the ridge by the time we reached 19,200 feet. We could see Archdeacons Tower and the snow-covered ridge which runs to the southwest from the Tower. There was another cornice at 19,500 feet, where the ridge from Archdeacons Tower intersected the ridge we were on. I referred to my pocket guide which I had copied from Washburn's guide to the Muldrow route. We turned slightly to the left, off the crest of the ridge, and passed two small ice humps mentioned in Washburn's guide. Ahead of us we could see a few wands and a trail leading to the crest of the Archdeacons Tower ridge. We were the first party of the year to climb via the Muldrow Glacier, but the West Buttress route joins the Muldrow route at Denali Pass. This trail had been packed into the snow by one of the West Buttress expeditions.

We reached the 19,550-foot crest of the Archdeacons Tower ridge at 16:06, where we stopped for a radio contact. Park headquarters had okayed our plan to fire a smoke bomb on the summit. Under our perfect weather conditions, the route ahead was plainly visible, a fine white line running across the vast flat area between the Archdeacons Tower ridge and the base of the summit slope. The trail stood out because it was a discordant line in this world of streamlined snow, its surface slightly higher or slightly lower than the surrounding snow. We could see the trail cutting diagonally leftward across the face of Kahiltna Spur, which is one of the three ridges that radiate outward from the centrally located summit. We knew that we had to gain the crest of Kahiltna Spur, then climb along that crest to the summit.

On the well-defined ridge above Denali Pass, we had placed no wands. Before us, the route stretched a quarter mile across a featureless snow plain to the base of Kahiltna Spur, then another quarter mile up a broad snow face to the crest of the summit ridge. By now we had fewer than twenty wands, and to have broken them in half would have been insufficient as well as ineffective. Wilcox kept six wands that he wanted for the summit, and we cached the few remaining ones beside some rocks which protruded from the snow of the Archdeacons Tower ridge. For our return from the summit we would have to rely on continuing good weather. In case of a partial whiteout, we would have to depend on finding our own tracks and the wands left by previous expeditions.

After sixteen minutes at 19,550 feet, we stepped off the ridge and descended a few feet onto the level snowfield. On the flat we ran into soft snow for the first time since leaving Denali Pass. We waded through a quarter mile of snow that was sometimes calf deep, and started up the slope of Kahiltna Spur.

The first few yards of the slope were covered by weak windcrust, requiring application of the frustrating climbing technique known as "two steps forward and one step back." This treadmill was tiring, and Lewis called for rest stops at intervals. We gained altitude steadily, and the slope became firm once again, permitting easy cramponing. The wands, which had been missing on the flat, were present again on the slope.

The weather was flawless, with motionless air and uninterrupted sunshine. Schlichter and I became so warm that we shed our shell parkas and down shirts, finding it perfectly comfortable to climb in our shirtsleeves. But to the west we could see cirrus clouds with hooked ends. These were "mares' tails," the harbingers of windstorms. Approximately twelve hours usually elapses between the appearance of mares' tails and the arrival of a windstorm.

Around 20,000 feet, we crossed the only crevasse that we had found on the entire route from Camp VII. The crevasse was a small one, only about two feet across, but we could not see the bottom of it. Another hundred feet of climbing brought us to the crest of the summit ridge. A fresh breeze hit us as soon as we topped the ridge, so Schlichter and I put our down shirts and shell parkas back on.

We reached the ridge crest at 18:00, and continued up the ridge toward the summit nine minutes later, after a brief radio check with Eielson Visitor Center. On this day the summit ridge was a thing of rare beauty, purest white against the deep blue sky, rippling and curling like a frozen wave. We climbed just to the left of the actual crest, because the right side dropped off 8,500 very sudden feet to the Kahiltna Glacier. The cornices on the ridge, although small, overhung this great chasm, and we wanted to be sure that we were walking well away from their potential lines of fracture.

The only sounds to be heard as I walked along the ridge were the breeze playing with my parka hood and the squeak of the cold, hard snow as it was pierced by my crampons. Schlichter and I were amazed by the ease with which we were climbing this ridge. We had expected to be gasping for breath in the thin, cold air, as indeed Lewis and Wilcox were. But we found it as pleasant as a climb along the wintery crest of one of our own Colorado Rockies.

During a brief rest stop, I walked cautiously to the very crest of the ridge and gazed summitward. Less than 100 yards ahead, the ridge took a 90° turn to the right, and just sixty feet past the turn was the summit! I was elated, and I shouted back to the others that I could see the summit, which was festooned with poles and wands. This moment was the climax of ten years of dreams and two years of planning and preparation. All that remained was an easy walk up the ridge to the top of the continent. As our rope moved up the ridge, each man stepped carefully to the crest where I had, and looked at the summit.

At 18:29, only twenty minutes after starting up the ridge crest, we crunched onto the summit of Mount McKinley, 20,320 feet in the frigid Alaskan air. We had to adjust to a new perspective; no more ridges or walls swept upward around us, everything sloped *down*. The summit was not corniced, so we stood on the very top and exchanged congratulations, back slaps, and bear hugs. Smiles were the order of the day, and Lewis's ice-coated beard could not hide a weary but wide grin.

Wilcox had left the radio switched on since our contact with the rangers from 20,100 feet, and the transmissions were recorded at Eielson. Wilcox's heavy breathing conveyed a vivid image of the rigors of high altitude to those who were listening to the radio at Eielson. As we reached the summit, Wilcox's comments kept Eielson informed of our progress: "Howard's on the summit now. Set to reel Jerry Lewis in. Real steep ridge up here. Now Paul's going in. Want to pull me in, Paul?" A long pause followed as we danced a crampon jig on the summit.

We stepped down onto a platform a few feet below the summit, to get out of the breeze. Then Wilcox continued: "This is Joe Wilcox on the summit of Mount McKinley."

Gordon Haber, one of the rangers at Eielson Visitor Center, replied: "Are you on top right now?"

Wilcox: "Roger, Roger. All four of us."

Haber: "Well, congratulations, congratulations."

Wilcox: "Ready to try that smoke bomb in a few minutes."

Haber: "Okay, we'll let you get your breath up there and then how about giving us a description. This is being recorded right now, we have a tape recorder goin'."

Wilcox: "This is Joe Wilcox of the Wilcox McKinley Expedition. We're on the summit of the mountain now. With me are Howard Snyder of the Colorado group, Paul Schlichter of the Colorado group, and Jerry Lewis of the Colorado group. The weather's just fine, some clouds at about seven thousand; high cirrus; we've been in the clear all day. Light breezes from the south, I guess. It's quite an exhilarating experience, we've all been planning this for years. We're climbing the mountain for different reasons, many of us, but we're all glad to be on top."

Most of us were climbing because we loved the beauty of the mountain wilderness, we enjoyed the company of good friends on a great adventure, and we relished the challenge of reaching the summit of this magnificent peak. But there were other reasons.

Our radio transmissions were being relayed via Park Service radio from Eielson to ranger Wayne Merry at Wonder Lake. Merry replied: "Well congratulations, Joe, and it's real good to hear you from up there. It's the first time we've talked to anybody on top of the mountain."

Although Merry could hear us, we were unable to hear him, so Haber passed Merry's congratulations along to us. I took the radio for a moment, to speak to Merry: "This is Howard Snyder. I want to say thanks very much for the assistance you gave us, and the advice. It's a beautiful day up here and we're sure glad to be here."

I handed the radio to Wilcox, and he continued: "We're not gonna really do much up here. Take a few pictures. I think we have a few banners. I have banners from all five of the universities I've been to and one from my home town at Neodesha, Kansas. And a flag from the State of Kansas, since I think I'm the first Kansan to climb Mount McKinley. And that's all I have to say, I send my greetings to everyone there, and I'll give the radio over to Howard."

Schlichter was standing on the very summit, a few feet above us, ready to fire the smoke bomb. Eielson reported that they had the peak in perfect view. The wind was blowing directly from Mount McKinley toward Eielson Visitor Center; conditions seemed ideal for the experiment. Schlichter yanked the ring on the flare, and a thin wisp of pale orange smoke curled upward from the canister. Within seconds a towering column of dense orange smoke was billowing from the flare, which Schlichter held like the Statue of Liberty's torch. The wind-driven smoke tumbled northeast toward Eielson. I called out on the radio: "Can you see us?"

More than thirty line-of-sight miles away, the rangers and visitors at Eielson saw us: "ten-four! We can see it! We can see it! ten-four! Oh, that's plain."

The Colorado group flares were double-ended, with a day flare (smoke) on one end, and a night flare (flame) on the other end. Schlichter fired off the night flare, but as we expected, it was not visible at Eielson. With the flare experiment successfully completed, we relaxed and enjoyed a Coca-Cola that Wilcox had saved for this occasion. I had a well-aged chunk of chocolate that I had carried to the summits of the peaks I had climbed in Switzerland and France. I passed it around, and we all had a gnaw at it.

Haber called on the radio, and told us that Ethyl Worthington, Lewis's next-door neighbor in Boulder, Colorado, was at Eielson Visitor Center. Lewis got on the radio: "Hello, this is Jerry Lewis on the summit. It's a bit chilly up here."

Miss Worthington replied: "I just took your picture. I just happened to be here at the time you reached the top." Miss Worthington offered to wire Lewis's family in Boulder and inform them that we had reached the top, an offer which was gratefully accepted.

Haber asked about temperature and wind conditions on the summit, and I replied: "The wind is about fifteen or twenty, with gusts up to twenty-five."

Haber: "Well, that doesn't sound too bad. Pretty cool up there?"

Snyder: "Actually it's very comfortable. I've got my heavy down gear in my pack. The temperature, we have just checked, is six degrees."

Haber: "Well, that isn't too bad at all. Boy, you guys hit it in beautiful weather."

Snyder: "Sure did. We're glad we started out today. It started out a little overcast and blowing snow, and we wanted to go anyway, but it sure turned into a beautiful day. If you want a little description from the summit here, Foraker is completely out of the clouds, the clouds are down about eleven thousand feet, and it looks beautiful. All the peaks off to the southeast are visible, the clouds are lying low in the valleys, and it's just a beautiful view up here."

Haber: "Well it sounds fantastic. I hope you're takin' a lotta pictures."

Haber then put George Robinson on the radio. Robinson had loaned his citizens' band radio to the Park Service, to be used by the Eielson rangers in communicating with our walkie-talkie units on the mountain.

Robinson: "I see you done pretty good. Glad you had some good communications anyway."

Wilcox: "We still have eight people to put up tomorrow."

Robinson: "Yeah, okay, I'll turn it back to Gordie now."

I winced a bit. Robinson had made a generous and beneficial contribution to us, people whom he had never met. It was typical Alaskan helpfulness, and I had hoped it would merit at least a "thank you."

Wilcox dictated a postcard over the radio, to be sent to his wife. This done, we signed off with Eielson and packed the radio away. Then we concentrated on surveying the world at our feet, a world that belonged to us for these few short moments.

To the north was McKinley's North Peak, 850 feet below us. To the east lay the Muldrow Glacier, our avenue to the summit. Also to the east, and 10,000 feet below, was a maze of glistening summits: Mt. Mather, Mt. Deception, Mt. Brooks, Mt. Tripyramid, and Mt. Silverthrone. On the south were peaks which we had seen for the first time when we reached the summit ridge, including 14,570-foot Mt. Hunter, and the ice-ribbed claw of 12,240-foot Mt. Huntington.

The western view was perhaps the most beautiful of all, looking along the sparkling ridge we had just ascended, and on to Mount Foraker, McKinley's 17,400-foot neighbor which stood in splendid isolation. No hills crowded around Foraker's base; it had plenty of room to stretch its feet into the surrounding glaciers.

In the midst of my summit photography, I was forced to change film, which was quite an experience under the conditions of wind and cold. With a fresh roll of film safely loaded, I took pictures of each one of us on the summit, and attempted to use the self-timer on my camera to get a group shot. The cold caused a malfunction, and the shutter jammed.

As we were preparing to start our descent, I buried a pack of matches on the summit. They were special to me because they were from the shop where I had worked while attending the University of Colorado. My employer had died just before I started my trip to Alaska. Inside the matchbook was written: "In memory of Walter E. Hickenbottom. The finest boss ever. Carried to the summit of Mount McKinley, Alaska, 20,320′, July 15th, 1967, by Howard H. Snyder."

We had been on top of the mountain for over an hour, and before we could start down we had to unsnarl the rope which had become tangled during our activities on the summit. At 19:53, after nearly one and a half superb hours on top, we began our descent.

At the front of the descending rope, Wilcox set a moderate pace, and we proceeded non-stop toward Denali Pass. At 20:00 we reached the point where we had first gained the summit ridge. The sun was shining through a veil of cirrus clouds, which had moved in from the southwest. We moved quickly down the face of Kahiltna Spur, plodded across the loose snow on the flat, and ascended the short slope to the Archdeacons Tower ridge. Elapsed time since leaving the summit was only thirty-nine minutes.

The wind, which we had not had to contend with since leaving the summit ridge, began to blow as we neared Denali Pass. The low clouds in the western valleys were starting to creep up the slopes, while the high clouds were descending toward the mountain tops.

When we reached 18,400 feet, I recognized the rocks where we had sat while making our first radio contact on the summit climb. Instead of going to the windward (west) side of the rocks where the snow was firm, Wilcox veered to the east. I heard Schlichter say to Wilcox, "Joe, we came up on the other side of these rocks." Wilcox did not answer, but kept going down the flank of the ridge, farther and farther from the crest.

The snow became deep and soft, and the layer just below the surface was splitting off in dangerous slabs. The soft snow was knee deep in places. Lewis and Wilcox were very tired, and they were slipping and floundering in the steep, loose snow. I shouted down to Wilcox, "Joe, let's get back up to the ridge." We waded slowly back to the crest of the ridge, then continued on to Denali Pass, arriving there at 21:30.

Wilcox was by now very fatigued, standing in what was to become his characteristic pose of exhaustion during the descent: head bowed and arms hanging limply at his side. We switched the rope around end-for-end, and I started breaking trail toward Camp VII, plowing through the drifted snow. Our trail from the morning had been obliterated, and many of the two-foot "mini wands" were already gone. We arrived in Camp VII at 21:53, exactly two hours after leaving the summit.

The men from Camp VI were arriving at Camp VII at the same time as we were. They were moving very slowly, about two rope lengths below the camp, and it was easy to see that they were having trouble. We dropped our packs in the camp and moved down the trail to meet the struggling team from Camp VI. Walt Taylor was leading, followed by Schiff, Steve Taylor, and Russell. Russell was very weak with sickness, and he had distributed part of his load to the others on the rope. Sticking from his pack was a flag, constructed from remnants of the burned tent's floor and lashed onto a ten-foot bamboo probe pole. In the crisp breeze which was now blowing, the flag added at least ten pounds to his load in the form of wind resistance. I took Russell's pack for him, while Lewis took the tent that S. Taylor was hand carrying, and we moved up to the camp. The entire expedition of twelve men was now at Camp VII.

Clark and McLaughlin had made no attempt on North Peak. They had spent the day resting in Camp VII, with Janes and Luchterhand. While the newly arrived team was setting up its Logan tent, Wilcox and Janes came into the Colorado group's tent to start preparing supper. This was chili night, and we decided to eat only the hamburger and tomato sauce, leaving out the chili beans and spices. It was the second gourmet's meal in two nights.

While supper was cooking, Janes massaged his back and commented, "When we get down, I want to sit in a chair with a back." Janes was afraid of the way the Wilcox group's stoves were behaving: "I don't like these stoves. You never know what they're going to do." When the cooking was finished, Janes pitched the stove out into the snow, without even closing the clamshell cover.

The wind increased, and the clouds began to wrap around the mountain. By midnight, a howling storm had enveloped Camp VII, and we were prisoners of the weather's whim.

8

THE STORMS
Inferno of Snow

High winds shrieked through Camp VII all day on 16 July, while fog and snow limited visibility to just a few yards. I estimated the wind to be gusting around 40 to 50 mph, and it was moving vast amounts of loose snow. I had had extensive experience in estimating wind speeds, partly because my home town of Boulder is often swept by extreme chinook winds with velocities over 100 mph. On several occasions I had climbed in winds which were officially clocked in excess of 100 mph. These experiences gave me a healthy respect for the power of a mountain wind, which can suffocate or freeze a climber even if it fails to rip him from his tracks and carry him away.

Climbing either up or down was impossible in this weather. If we had harbored any doubts as to the identity of the mountain king, the storm dispelled them. Weather rules the upper slopes of Mount McKinley. A more brutal dictator can not be imagined.

The wind-driven snow hit our tent with tremendous force, and

112

raced up the sidewall in waves. We were being sandblasted with hard, dry snow. When the wind was at maximum velocity, the friction of the snow sliding over our nylon tent generated an astonishingly large electrical charge in the fabric, resulting in a continuous stinging spark which jumped from the tent walls to our bodies. If we moved an arm, or leg, or shoulder away from the tent walls, the spark merely jumped instead to our backs. There was no escaping it.

We could not know how long the storm would last, but we made plans to move down to the 15,000-foot camp when possible. We spent the day of the sixteenth sleeping, or at least resting in our sleeping bags. I took my camera into my sleeping bag and managed to thaw out the self-timer, thus unjamming the shutter. Schlichter and I experienced our only altitude effect on this day: while resting and breathing normally, we would occasionally give a deep, involuntary sigh. This was an attempt by our bodies to wring a bit more oxygen out of the rarefied air.

We were looking forward to dinner that night. The beef stew menu had come up, and it was the Wilcox group's best meal. When dinnertime rolled around, the food was cooked in the Logan tent, and the Colorado group was somehow forgotten. We had no beef stew that night. Lewis said that he was getting weak and sick from lack of proper food. We hoped tomorrow's weather would permit us to descend to 15,000 feet, where the Colorado group's food and equipment were cached.

Just as had happened on our summit day, the wind and snow abated somewhat at mid-morning on 17 July. We were eager to get moving, but somewhat reluctant to leave the cozy warmth of our sleeping bags. As Schlichter crawled out of his sleeping bag, he said, "The beautiful butterfly emerges from its cocoon." Schlichter and I went outside to dig out our equipment and start packing our loads for the descent.

Lewis's condition had worsened overnight. Always the last with the least when it came to critical comments, Schlichter nonetheless said, "Jerry is working at about twenty per cent efficiency today." A little later we heard Lewis stirring in the tent. He bolted for the door, and just managed to get his head outside before he vomited. I shoveled off our doorstep.

Wilcox was also ill, and he would accompany us down to Camp VI, where we would wait for the second summit team. Clark, as deputy leader of the expedition, was to be in charge of the second summit team.

I had seen Russell vomiting that morning, and I asked him indirectly if he wanted to go down: "John, does anybody in your tent want to go down?" Russell was incensed by the very suggestion, and he replied gruffly, "No! Nobody wants to go down!" Schiff took exception to this blanket statement, and said he would go down with us.

Wilcox was too sick and weak to pack up his own tent, so W. Taylor and Luchterhand dug the two-man mountaineer tent out of the snow, folded it up, and packed Wilcox's pack for him. Lewis was in a similar condition. He stood in front of our tent, looking lost. His bare hands were covered by a thin coat of wind-driven snow, while his down mittens dangled at his side from their keeper strings.

I asked gently, "Jerry, why don't you put your mittens on?"

"They're full of snow," came the bewildered reply.

I brushed the snow off Lewis's hands, then took off my mittens and warmed his hands in my own. I shook the snow out of his mitts and slipped them on his hands. Schlichter put Lewis's crampons on for him, and we were nearly ready to start our descent.

By 11:00, McLaughlin, Janes, W. Taylor, and Luchterhand were out of their tents, preparing for their summit climb. Luchterhand was apparently recovered from his illness of two days before. He said that he was going to carry his sleeping bag to the summit, as a safety precaution in case of a forced bivouac.

The wind was still blowing at about 20 mph, and thin clouds were still present. McLaughlin tried to get Clark to start packing for the climb, but Clark was not convinced that the time had arrived. He declared, "I'm not going to go dashing off until I know what the weather is going to do," and he stayed in his tent.

While Schlichter and I took down our tent, Lewis talked with S. Taylor. Taylor had also been ill, although his symptoms were not obvious as was the case with Wilcox, Lewis, and Russell. Lewis asked Taylor how he was feeling, and Taylor replied with a rather noncommittal, "Oh, sometimes I feel all right, sometimes I don't feel too good."

Lewis asked specifically if Taylor wanted to come with the descending party, and he replied, "No, I think I'll stay up here with the rest of the guys."

McLaughlin discussed the route to the summit with me, since he thought he would probably be breaking trail for the team. I pointed out the rocks along the ridge above Denali Pass, and advised him to stay on the crest of the ridge, where the wind had removed any loose snow. My finger traced the route up the ridge to Archdeacons Tower. I mentioned the ridge which was behind the Tower, and indicated that the route crossed a large flat area, and then ascended the face of Kahiltna Spur to the summit ridge. Lastly, I told him that the route was wanded only as far as Denali Pass, and only with half-size wands at that. We had followed tracks and red plastic wands from 19,400 feet on up, I said, and if the weather was good the second team could do the same.

I mentioned the wands which we had left at 19,550 feet, and told McLaughlin to take enough wands to mark their route, since the rest of the wands had come up with the last party from Camp VI. All of these comments seemed to me to be easy enough to remember, but I was describing what was for me familiar terrain. To McLaughlin, however, it was all new, and only as familiar as his map could make it.

McLaughlin thought that their party would make a rapid climb, and maybe be able to descend the next day all the way from Camp VII at 17,900 feet to the Muldrow Glacier. "You be ready to start down Karstens tomorrow morning," he said.

I hoped that they could make such good time, but I had serious doubts. "That'd be fine if we could move all the way down to the Muldrow tomorrow." Then I continued, "But you're gonna have some pretty tired people when you get back here. We may have to spend another night at 15,000."

"Yeah," McLaughlin replied, "but we'll try to get it all done tomorrow if we can."

Clark had contacted Eielson three times that morning, using up the precious reserves of energy in the radio's batteries. He finished his third contact at about 11:15, and put the radio in his pack. Clark emerged from his tent, and after watching Lewis for a while, he motioned to me. I walked over, and Clark handed me some stimulant pills from his personal first aid kit. "In case Jerry needs them," he said.

"We've got Dexadrine for that, Jerry," I answered.

"Yes," Clark insisted, "but these are milder. They might do some good."

"Okay, thanks," I said, and stuffed the pills into my pocket.

I took our rope out of my pack, and Schlichter, Lewis, and I roped up. With Wilcox and Schiff in our party, we needed more than the 150-foot Colorado group rope for the descent. We found Wilcox's rope buried in the snow, tangled with McLaughlin's in a frozen mess. McLaughlin and I untangled the ropes, and Wilcox and Schiff tied in. Wilcox, Schiff, and Lewis were all weak, and I wanted more than one strong man to a team, so we tied the two ropes together, making an unwieldy 270-foot rope.

We were just about ready to go now, and Schlichter took one last look around Camp VII. He gazed up at North Peak, and recalled that I had said we would climb it if the weather was good, and if we had sufficient food and fuel left, and if people wanted to climb it. Schlichter observed: "The weather's bad, we're low on food, and nobody wants to. Otherwise all the conditions are fulfilled."

The men of the summit team were nearly ready to begin their ascent, which we understood they would be doing momentarily. Just now they were busily digging around the camp in search of two liters of fuel that had been buried in the snow three days before. Unlike our procedure in previous camps, the loads carried to Camp VII had not been placed in a single, designated area, but rather just dumped at random near the various tents.

With shouts of "See ya tomorrow!" we started down the trail at one minute until noon. We progressed steadily downward, despite the chore of breaking trail through the drifted snow, and were soon past the upper icefall. The weather had become absolutely perfect, with brilliant sunshine, a cloudless sky, and not the slightest breeze. It was even better than our summit day.

As we slogged along on the flat between the upper and central icefalls, Lewis and Schiff began calling rest stops. No sooner would we stop than Lewis, Schiff, and Wilcox would collapse to the ground. By 13:00, we had reached the equipment cache at 16,500 feet. An avalanche had occurred sometime since 14 July, sweeping down from the walls of North Peak and crossing our trail just 200 feet from the cache.

Since I was carrying the tent, Schlichter took the three-day Colorado group food bag from the cache and lashed it to his pack. Three Wilcox group food bags and three pairs of snowshoes were left undisturbed. While Schlichter worked at the cache, the three sick men sat in the snow, their energies spent, their postures bent with exhaustion.

The top of the central icefall was at an elevation of 16,400 feet, and here our trail cut sharply to the left toward the wall of North Peak, to skirt the edge of the icefall. Once past this corner we would be unable to see the high camp. I turned for a look upglacier, and was surprised by what I saw. More than an hour had passed since we left Camp VII, and yet we could see the climbers walking around in the camp. I called back to Schlichter, "Look at that! They're still in camp!" We started around the bend in the trail; the high camp and the men of the summit team passed out of sight. We never saw them again.

Many wands along our route had been blown away during the previous day's storm, and not a single wand remained here at the 16,400-foot corner. Unable to find the right-angle turn, we cut diagonally across the corner, toward the edge of the glacier. Just behind me on the rope, Schlichter yelled "Whoa!" as his foot broke through a covered crevasse that I had missed. Then his leg plunged in up to thigh depth, and he exclaimed, "I'm in!" I fell to an ice ax arrest position, but Schlichter managed to extricate himself without help. I asked him if we should back up and find a slightly different route, but he said that the crevasse was small enough for the other men to step across, so we continued our descent.

At 15,900 feet, on the slope beside the central icefall, Lewis called for another rest stop. After a few minutes, I asked, "Ready, Jerry?" Lewis rose wearily to his feet. Schiff and Wilcox were still sitting, but I knew that Wilcox would be ready to move when the others were ready. I called out to Schiff, "C'mon, Anshel. Let's go." Schiff replied, "Joe isn't up yet."

Schlichter, seeing the comic possibilities of an endless stalemate, turned to me with an imaginary dialog: " 'Let's go, Joe.' 'But Anshel isn't up yet.' "

Slowly, slowly, we descended the gentle section of the Harper Glacier above our 15,000-foot campsite. At 15:00 we reached Camp VI and started setting up the tents. We cleared the cache off our tent platform, and found that the last team to leave the camp had moved most of the Colorado group's gear out of the cache, using Schlichter's poncho to cover their own equipment. In order to construct his flag from the fabric of the burned tent, Russell had opened the Colorado group first aid kit and used the entire supply of adhesive tape. In the process, the scissors, razor blade, needle, and band-aids had been lost from the kit.

With the camp set up, we turned to cooking. Vast quantities of fluids and Colorado group food were prepared, and we ate our fill of everything. Lewis seemed to be back to normal after just a few hours of rest and a good meal. The weather was phenomenally mild and calm throughout the afternoon, so we did our cooking outside. The sun slipped behind North Peak at 18:00, and the temperature dropped drastically, although the sky remained clear and windless.

That evening, our regular 20:00 radio contact was scheduled with Eielson, so I walked over to Wilcox's tent to listen in. Wilcox and Schiff were inside their tent. Since it was definitely a two-man tent, I stood outside.

The sky above us was still clear blue and calm, but a look upglacier revealed a soft blanket of cloud on the summit ridge. It looked as though the mountain had put a cotton shawl on its shoulders to ward off the evening chill. The cloud was a strange motionless veil that covered the summit, Archdeacons Tower, and the upper part of the ridge above Denali Pass. The route to the summit was obscured by the merest of margins: Farthing Horn and the lowest rocks of Archdeacons Tower were barely visible; Denali Pass and the ridge just above it were in the clear. It was the margin between success and disaster.

Eielson came on the air, and we read them loud and clear. Our five-watt transceiver (unit one) was with the summit team, while at Camp VI we were using the three-watt rig (unit two). Due to some oddity in radio conditions, unit one and unit two were unable to hear one another, while Eielson could communicate with both field units. Eielson relayed messages between units one and two.

Clark's team, unable to see the upper part of the mountain because of the cloud cap, asked if there was a large cornice on the summit. Wilcox replied to Eielson, "Roger, Roger."

I said, "There's no cornice on the summit, Joe."

Wilcox answered brusquely, "The summit *I* was on was corniced." So the word went out to the summit team that there was a large cornice on the summit.

At Eielson, Haber relayed the "Roger" to Clark's team. Clark replied: "Okay, ETA approximately forty-five minutes to one hour, Gordie." Haber told Clark to give a call on the radio when they got within a hundred or so feet of the summit, so that Haber could monitor and record the conversation for the last few feet to the top. Clark answered: "Pretty cold for that, but we'll see what happens, Gordie. We'll try and give you a call. KHD6990 unit one, clear."

I went back to our tent. Wilcox continued talking with Haber on the radio. He asked what was going on with the summit team, and Haber informed him that they figured they were forty-five minutes to an hour from the top. Wilcox shouted the news across to our tent. Wilcox then asked Haber if all seven men from the high camp were in the summit team. Haber thought not: "The way I understood it, there was one of the seven that got a little sick, I guess, and couldn't quite make it, so I guess he went back down with some of the others that were goin' back down to 15,000 camp. Right now, I assume there's six."

Wilcox answered: "There's no one ill here. We have Anshel Schiff, who did not attempt the summit. But there should be one other climber at 17–9 camp who did not attempt the summit today. I was just wondering who it was."

Haber said he would ask Clark about it the next time he contacted unit one. Wilcox said he would turn on the radio in about a half an hour, to monitor the summit team's transmission from the top. He turned off the radio, and the silence of an arctic night enfolded the camp.

The second summit team had spent quite a long time in Camp VII on the afternoon of 17 July, not starting for the summit at noon as we had thought they were. Russell and S. Taylor were ill, and some of the other men had been weakened by the altitude. Despite McLaughlin's hopes to the contrary, the team was expecting a slow climb. As a precaution against a forced bivouac, each man packed his sleeping bag for the summit climb.

Before the team was ready to leave Camp VII, S. Taylor decided he was too weak and ill to make the summit climb. He told them that he would stay in camp and await their return. Perhaps the climbers lost additional precious minutes of good weather in arranging the camp for Taylor's solitary vigil.

Shortly after 15:00, Clark's team started up the trail toward Denali Pass, which was less than an hour's march away even for a slowly moving party. At 16:40, Clark stopped for a radio contact with Eielson. He reported that they were just above Denali Pass. Clark gave a summit ETA of 20:00 to 21:00. He estimated the wind at about 15 mph, and the temperature somewhere between zero and ten degrees. It was another fine day, but they had lost three hours of perfect weather by not starting for the summit at noon. Those three hours were the vanguard of eternity.

By radio-contact time at 20:00, Clark's team was peering up the ridge into thickening fog. Clark asked about a cornice on the summit, and after receiving an affirmative (and erroneous) reply, he estimated they were within one hour of the summit. If the cornice they were seeing had been on the summit ridge, then they would have been less than thirty minutes from the top, since the summit ridge cornices can only be seen from the ridgetop itself. But in fact, the men were not to reach the summit for yet another fifteen energy-sapping, bone-chilling hours. Where were they?

Other than those on the summit ridge, the only cornices on the route were at 19,100 and 19,500 feet on the ridge above Denali Pass. The men were above 19,000 feet on the ridge, and on the fog-dimmed skyline they could see the large cornice at 19,500 feet, which hung from the west end of the Archdeacons Tower ridge. Clark's party mistook this corniced point for the summit. After the radio contact, they continued on their way up the ridge.

The ridge broadened and became quite gentle around 19,200 feet, then the route turned leftward toward Archdeacons Tower. At 19,400 feet, Clark encountered the first of the red plastic wands which the first summit team had followed. The wands led to the top of the Archdeacons Tower ridge, but there were none leading out across the flat toward Kahiltna Spur. The wind ripping across the flat had removed the wands from the loose snow even before the first summit team's climb.

Around 22:00, Clark's team reached the crest of the Archdeacons Tower ridge, at 19,550 feet. By now the fog was dense, and the lighting poor. The men could not see the flat ahead of them, nor could they see the summit which loomed beyond the flat. They thought perhaps they had reached the summit ridge. If they consulted their maps at all, it was easy to convince themselves that the gentle slope they had ascended above 19,200 feet was the level area indicated on the map at 19,500 feet. The leftward curve of the trail as it ascended the flank of the Archdeacons Tower ridge was analogous to the upward-leftward traverse across the face of Kahiltna Spur. The ridge they were on must therefore be the summit ridge, or so they hoped.

Nagged by doubt, and unable to see their route ahead or even their surroundings, they put in a radio call to Eielson. Haber acknowledged their call, and Clark said: "Gordie, we've got real problems up here. Do you have any method to contact unit two?" Haber tried to contact us, but was unsuccessful. "What's the problem?" he asked.

Clark related their difficulties: "Well, this route is not well wanded at all. We've lost the wands, and so we're floundering around. We don't know whether we're on the summit ridge or not, we don't know whether the summit ridge is supposed to be wanded or not. And visibility is something else. We think we're pretty close to the summit, but we can't tell. We're just floundering around in the dark here. Visibility is about three hundred feet."

The radio reception was fuzzy, and Haber asked for a repeat. Clark repeated some of the message, and Haber understood a bit more.

Haber asked for one more repeat, and Clark replied: "The situation is that we have followed the wands to what we think may be the summit ridge, if we can find one more wand."

Haber still could not catch the entire message, and he asked for two more repeats. Clark finally said: "We have cold batteries, we have cold batteries." Haber suggested that they try to warm the batteries, then give him another call in a few minutes. Clark replied with a "Roger." Haber got on the Park Service radio, and advised Wayne Merry of the situation.

Haber heard a call from Clark at 22:45, and he acknowledged the call. Clark said: "Eielson, this is unit one." Haber answered, but nothing further was heard from unit one. He called repeatedly, but was unable to contact Clark's team again that night.

The climbers of the summit team were faced with the most important decision they would ever make. They were without communications, and hemmed in by fog and darkness. Several were cold and weak; they knew if they descended to Camp VII they would be unable to return to the summit. Also, unless they had marked it on their ascent, the route down was marked by only a very few wands. They may have thought it would take a long time to find the top of the ridge to Denali Pass. They were all carrying sleeping bags: this was the deciding factor. Anywhere else on the climb, the idea of bivouacking would have met derision and rejection: "I'm going back to camp where we've got tents, and food, and stoves." But here, at 19,550 feet, with the summit almost in their grasp, the decision was made to bivouac, and tomorrow to be done with this mountain and go home.

The summit team had no tents, and no shovel with which to dig a snow cave—the night would be spent in the open. There were no stoves; hence there would be no warm drinks to drive off the chill and prevent dehydration. The men sought what little shelter they could find, most likely behind the rocks at the west end of the Archdeacons Tower ridge, or by digging into the loose snow on the flanks of the ridge. Then they settled down to spend a miserable night, high in the frozen Alaskan sky.

°   °   °

The eighteenth of July dawned clear and calm at Camp VI. The glacier above us was free of cloud, and the summit stood unobscured on the skyline. We assumed that the second summit team was in Camp VII, and would soon be coming down to join us. The Colorado men spent the day checking through all of their food supplies, selecting the delicacies to be carried on the descent, and caching the remainder. We planned to carry three complete days of food in addition to the selected goodies, and to pick up a three-day Colorado group food bag at the 13,000-foot Coxcomb cache. The Wilcox group's food caches and two other small Colorado group caches were also on our descent route.

By mid-morning, a cloud cap once again covered the summit, and clouds started moving downglacier toward our camp. A heavy snowfall began at noon, driven down the mountain's slopes by the whiplash of a stinging wind. Throughout the day, we were expecting to hear the ring of voices and the crunch of boots on the snow as the summit team came down the trail to join us. But we heard only the howling wind.

We began to wonder what was delaying Clark's team, and we found out during our radio contact that night. Eielson informed us that the summit team had reached the top at 11:30 that morning, after a bivouac on the night of the seventeenth. Clark did not make radio contact on the night of the eighteenth, and we surmised that the men were in Camp VII, too busy tending to their hunger, dehydration, and fatigue to remember the radio schedule.

The wind had blown continuously since noon, and we were lulled to sleep that night by its monotonous roar.

The fog had begun to dissipate on the morning of 18 July, and through the mist the men of Clark's team could see the summit glowing in the pale light of sunrise. Anyone who has spent a forced bivouac in below-zero cold and piercing wind can confirm that it is no easy task to start moving again in the morning. It is not a simple matter of standing up and starting along the trail. The men of the summit team, some dangerously weak even before the bivouac, were further debilitated by a sleepless night of shivering and labored breathing in the wretchedly thin, cold air. Every movement was an effort, and some of the climbers were likely suffering from frostbitten feet. Clark and McLaughlin were wearing leather expedition boots of the double-boot type. Despite the high-quality double construction of their boots, both men had gotten cold feet while using them lower on the mountain. Russell was wearing felt boots, and the rest of the men were wearing rubber "K" (Korean) boots.

The summit was showing more clearly every minute, as the sun burned off the fog. Russell was in no shape to continue the climb. He would wait on the trail at 19,550 feet, while the summit party "dashed" to the top and back.

The climbing team, now five in number, prepared for the final assault on the summit. With W. Taylor in the lead, they started across the flat toward Kahiltna Spur. As they ascended the face, clouds slithered up the peak from the west, and once again they were in a whiteout. But they had been able to scan the route all the way to the summit during the clear hours of the morning, so they knew where to head. The trail was much easier to follow on the face, since it was not buried by drifting snow as was the flat, and quite a few wands were still in place on this part of the route. At the top of the face they met the summit ridge. All that remained was to follow the ridge to the top of the mountain.

Weary and cold, the climbers cramponed onto the summit at 11:30. They were glad to be on top at last, but they had no desire to stay there very long. Clark called Eielson on the radio. Haber replied: "What happened last night? You called about a quarter to eleven, I guess, and I heard your call and I answered, but you didn't acknowledge. I thought maybe you got radio trouble."

Clark: "We probably didn't copy you. We had some weak batteries, in fact they're still weak right now. We ended up bivouacking as a matter of fact. It got so fogged in that we couldn't go up and we couldn't go down."

Haber: "Well, you're comin' in loud and clear right here now. How long do you plan on staying on top?"

Clark: "Oh, five or ten more minutes, Gordie. Kinda cold up here."

Clark handed the radio over to McLaughlin, who dictated a postcard to his parents: "Dear Mom and Dad. Radio from the summit. A-okay. See you in a week or two. Love, Mark." Haber copied the message, then asked what the view was like on the summit.

McLaughlin replied: "The view consists of four other guys at the moment." Four other guys: there were only five on the summit. "That's all, it's completely whited out. We're just below the summit. You can see the wands on the summit and that's all."

Haber: "Well, you didn't luck out like the last four, I guess. They had a real good view when they were up there. Do you mind just naming off the people that are up there right now?"

McLaughlin: "Jerry Clark, Hank Janes, Dennis Luchterhand, Mark McLaughlin. Oh, and Walt Taylor, wouldn't want to forget him, he led all the way up." McLaughlin had been very careful not to miss anyone. Russell was not with the summit team.

Haber, not noticing that only five names had been called off, then mentioned that Wilcox had wondered where the seventh man was. McLaughlin answered: "Seventh man is Steve Taylor. He didn't feel good at all, so he stayed in camp at 17–9. He's probably wondering where we are at the moment."

Haber said he would relay the message to Wilcox, and asked if the summit team had anything more to say. McLaughlin replied: "All five of us got to the summit at exactly the same time." All five.

The transmission started growing weaker, so the summit team prepared to sign off. After agreeing to contact Eielson at the usual 20:00 radio check, McLaughlin said: "Thanks very much. KHD6990, unit one, clear." They were never heard from again.

Clark's team signed off its last radio transmission at 11:45 on 18 July, and started its descent. At noon, the snow began to fall and the wind began to blow in our camp at 15,000 feet. By the time the summit team reached the flat at 19,500 feet, the wind was blowing at least 30 to 40 mph, whipping blinding sheets of snow into the men's faces. The climbers trudged across the seemingly interminable flat, struggling to find the route, fighting the wind for every breath and every glimpse of the route ahead. They finally reached the Archdeacons Tower ridge, their bivouac site of the night before. If Russell was still waiting there and was able to walk, he was tied into one of the ropes. Then the team started downward into the raging whiteout.

They moved straight down the slope, not veering left toward the top of the ridge to Denali Pass. This was done either because the men had lost the route completely; or because they were trying to descend straight to Camp VII, avoiding the wind-blasted ridge to Denali Pass. At 19,400 feet, they left the gentle shelf of Archdeacons Tower and started down the steepening slope. They were marking their route, and one of their wands was later found in place on this slope. The wind was increasing steadily, and the slope was fearfully steep considering the weather and the physical condition of the climbers. A halt was called.

Retreat was cut off now; it was probably beyond the endurance of even healthy men to force a way through the blinding and suffocating storm, and certainly beyond the endurance of these weakened men. They had no choice, they must bivouac for yet another night below Archdeacons Tower, in sleeping bags already icy from the night before. Perhaps they tried to dig a hole in which they could take refuge from the wind's unceasing barrage, but it would have been a shallow shelter at best, since they had only ice axes and weary hands to use as tools. They huddled together for what little warmth and protection that could afford, and were soon covered by the drifting snow.

In Camp VI, heavy snowfall continued all day on 19 July, accompanied by a constant wind. We could not see up the glacier, and no one came down from the high camp. The summit team must be sitting out the storm at Camp VII, waiting for a weather break to allow them to move down the mountain. Or so we thought.

That evening, I was once again standing outside Wilcox's tent during the 20:00 radio contact with Eielson. For the second consecutive night unit one failed to make contact with Eielson, and we began to have serious worries, envisioning the high camp full of sick men with a non-functioning radio. Wilcox proposed that he, Schlichter, and I start for the high camp that evening to check on the situation. I said that I thought it would be best if we waited until morning. From inside his tent, and likely huddled in his sleeping bag as well, Wilcox retorted,

"What's the matter? You've made the summit and now you don't want to go up any more?"

Standing outside in the wind, I looked up the glacier into the dark gray fog, with the wind-driven snow peppering my eyes and stinging my face. "Look, Joe," I replied, "the weather's no good for it now. The wind and snow are too heavy. And it's getting dark at night now, in case you hadn't noticed." Wilcox agreed to wait until morning to start for Camp VII, and we settled down for what little rest we could get that night.

The wind's buffeting of our tent lessened at about 06:00 on the morning of 20 July. I poked my head out of the tent and looked upglacier. An impenetrable cloud layer hung at 16,000 feet, at the top of the central icefall, but the snow was falling lightly now, and the wind was only about 20 mph. I shouted across to Wilcox's tent, "Joe! The wind's down now! Let's get going!"

Schlichter and I ate a hurried breakfast of leftover Jello and fruit, then packed our clothing and sleeping bags for the climb to the high camp. Wilcox filled a pressure cooker with gasoline for use in the stove in Camp VI. About two gallons of gas remained in the five-gallon can, and this he packed to carry to Camp VII. Schlichter had no faith in the Wilcox group's stoves, so he packed a Colorado group stove, kerosene, and alcohol to carry to the high camp.

We started up the trail at 06:30, leaving Lewis and Schiff in camp in the Colorado group tent. The wind started to increase almost as soon as we left camp, and the snow began to fall more heavily. Soon we were climbing face-on into the blast of a snow-laden wind which was gusting up to 40 mph. Our trail was completely drifted over, but we were quickly made aware if we strayed off it. As long as we kept on the trail, our snowshoes sunk in about six inches, but when we stepped off the trail, we plummeted in to knee depth. After several episodes of thrashing in the deep snow, we learned to keep on the trail by taking small steps, testing each one before putting full weight on it.

The wind intensified, and the cloud ceiling dropped in right on top of us. We stood still for minutes at a time, straining to see the wands ahead. When the wands came into view during momentary lulls, first one, then two, then three, we memorized their positions and plodded onward. Before I could cover the seventy-five-foot distance between Schlichter and myself, his tracks would be obliterated.

Conditions were rapidly becoming intolerable, and progress was pitifully slow. Schlichter and I knew our chances of reaching the high camp were almost nil, but we said nothing, and moved on. We thought the summit team was at Camp VII, perhaps in dire need of help. Wilcox would have to make the painful decision to return to Camp VI. At 09:00, Wilcox stopped where the trail crossed a two-foot high ice bump, the only break in the otherwise smooth surface of the Harper Glacier between our camp and the central icefall. Schlichter and I moved up to Wilcox, and he proceeded to contact Eielson on the radio. Wilcox described the conditions we were encountering, and asked for a weather forecast. As usual, Eielson had no forecast, but said they would have one for us in time for the 20:00 contact.

We had covered three-quarters of a mile of gentle glacier in two and a half hours. We were doing slightly better than a quarter of a mile per hour. In an indirect manner, Wilcox announced the unavoidable decision to turn back. He opened his pack and pulled out the gasoline can. "We'll leave it here on the trail," he said, "so we can pick it up when we come back up." We returned to the 15,000-foot camp, one slow and careful step at a time.

As we entered camp, Schiff anxiously popped his head out of the tent. He had hoped the clatter of snowshoes meant the return of the summit team. Wilcox and Schiff returned to their two-man tent, while Schlichter and I crawled back into the Colorado group tent. And there we lay all morning, as the wind drummed at the tent walls and the snow continued to fall, hoping, praying to hear voices or footsteps on the trail above camp. In the early afternoon, the sky cleared completely and we could see the summit, but the wind continued without letup. During the late afternoon the clouds closed in again. "Winds got worse in evening," reads my logbook. We were experiencing winds in excess of 50 mph by the evening of 20 July.

Wilcox came over to our tent at 20:00 for the radio contact with Eielson. He had something important to say, and he wanted us to be in on it. Once in contact with Eielson, he began talking about a rescue operation. At Eielson, Haber put in a call on the Park radio, and informed Wayne Merry. With Eielson as a go-between, Wilcox and Merry discussed the possibility of a rescue for the men we assumed to be at Camp VII. They finally decided to ask bush pilot Don Sheldon to make an overflight of the high camp, to determine the condition of the men who were thought to be there.

After the radio contact, Wilcox returned to his tent, and we spread out our sleeping bags. Our circumstances gave rise to a completely impromptu group recitation. As we nestled into the sleeping bags, Lewis said, "Now I lay me down to sleep."

I continued, "I pray the Lord my soul to keep."

Schlichter added the next line, "If I die before I wake."

I concluded, "I pray the Lord my soul to take."

The clear skies that afternoon had lasted for three hours. I had repeatedly thrust my head out of the tent and scanned the route above us, hoping to see the summit team descending. We could not climb uphill into the face of the wind, but I had thought that perhaps with clear skies, and the wind at their backs, Clark's team could descend. But we had seen nothing. Perhaps if we had looked to the northern slopes of Archdeacons Tower we would have seen two minute orange specks in an infinity of whiteness, falling, struggling, moving downward.

The summit team began its second bivouac on the afternoon of 18 July. The storm held the climbers in an iron grip, and it would not relent. There was no letup on the nineteenth; heavy snowfall and slashing wind, visibility zero. The men clung to the treacherous slope, battered by the wind, gnawed by the cold. All were suffering from some degree of frostbite by now. But the terrible pain had ceased in some of the men's hands and feet, which were frozen beyond feeling.

The morning of 20 July offered little hope, but toward noon the clouds began to thin out, and before long the mountain was clear. The men had eaten nothing other than some high-energy candy bars in the past three days. They had had neither warm food nor drink, and had spent three days exposed to the most savage weather conditions to be

Approaching Camp VI, 15,000 feet. Left to right on the skyline: Farthing Horn, Archdeacons Tower, Denali Pass.

Aftermath of the tent fire. Left to right: McLaughlin, W. Taylor, Russell.

Seracs in the central Harper Icefall.

Camp VII, 17,900 feet. Leaving for the summit on 15 July. Left to right: Schlichter, Wilcox, Lewis.

Snyder at 18,800 feet on the ridge above Denali Pass. *Photo by Jerry M. Lewis.*

Cornice at 19,100 feet, overlooking the Kahiltna Glacier.

Mount Foraker, 17,400 feet, as seen from 20,000 feet on Kahiltna Spur. The clouds with hooked ends are "mare's tails."

The summit ridge. Summit on the right.

On the summit ridge at 20,100 feet, Mount Foraker in the background. Near to far: Lewis, Schlichter, Wilcox (making radio contact).

The final few feet. Snyder approaching the summit. *Photo by Paul M. Schlichter*

On the summit. Left to right:
Lewis, Schlichter, Wilcox, Snyder.
Photo of Snyder by Jerry M. Lewis

View from the summit. Peaks to the southeast, including Mount Mather (in the distance), and Mount Silverthrone.

View from the summit southward to the Pacific Ocean, looking across McKinley's South Buttress to Mount Huntington.

Mount Foraker, 17,400 feet, from the summit of Mount McKinley.

Schlichter holding the summit
flare, Lewis at right.

The first summit team descending from the high camp on 17 July.

View upglacier from Camp VI at 15,000 feet, at 18:00 on 17 July. Left to right on the skyline: South summit and Farthing Horn, Archdeacons Tower, Denali Pass. Lewis standing next to tent.

View upglacier from Camp VI at 15,000 feet, at 20:00 on 17 July. The obscuring cloud moved in to cover the uppermost slopes of the mountain at this time.

Descent from Camp VI, 23 July. Near to far: Wilcox, Lewis, Schiff, Schlichter.

found anywhere on earth. Now the mountain was clear, but the wind raged on. About 1,500 feet below, the bright red and orange tents of Camp VII were visible, less than a mile away.

Those men who were still able rose from the snow. There may have been only two left by now who could accomplish this task—almost certainly W. Taylor and probably Luchterhand, who had been the Wilcox group's strongest climbers. They started moving straight down the slope, alone and unroped, heading directly for Camp VII. They carried only their sleeping bags; all else had likely been swept away during the bivouac.

The slope became increasingly steep, and the men began to encounter the crevasses which abound on the northern flank of Archdeacons Tower. Some of the men may have fallen into these crevasses, but two were able to avoid them and keep moving downward. One man had reached approximately the 19,100-foot level; the other was near 18,800 feet. Then, after three hours of clear weather, the clouds enveloped the peak once again. The climbers leaned back against the slope to rest. Alone, their last desperate chance now gone, the men relinquished the fragile thread of life.

Steve Taylor had remained in Camp VII at 17,900 feet, to await the return of the summit team. He had no radio, no way to find out what was happening to any of the eleven others in the expedition, and no way to inform anyone of his own situation. Taylor had expected the summit team to return to Camp VII on the evening of 17 July. By the morning of the eighteenth, Taylor was beginning to wonder and worry. At some time between 18 and 20 July, Taylor hiked downglacier toward our camp at 15,000 feet. He most likely made this hike on the morning of 18 July, utilizing the clear weather that prevailed until the summit clouds moved down and covered Camp VII just before noon; or during the three clear hours on the afternoon of the twentieth. Taylor's ice ax was found at about 17,400 feet, near the top of the upper icefall. It may have been blown part of that distance across the smooth, hard snow by winds that certainly exceeded 100 mph at the height of the storm.

The flag and flagpole that Russell had improvised were found about 150 yards downglacier from the high camp. The pole was standing vertically, and had obviously been placed there by someone. Taylor's sleeping bag was draped loosely around the base of the pole. Taylor had either hung his sleeping bag there to serve as a distress signal (although better things for that purpose were available); or by a million-to-one chance, the flagpole had caught the bag as it was blown out of Camp VII.

Finding himself unable to make the descent to Camp VI, Taylor returned to the high camp. The foggy, snowy hours became a blur, pushed along by the roaring disharmony of the wind. The eighteenth and nineteenth went by, the twentieth arrived. Still no companions returned, the wind and snow continued without moderation. Three hours of clear sky on the afternoon of 20 July might have given rise to hope, but it was false hope. The clouds closed in again, and the wind rose to a new crescendo. Taylor's Logan tent shook so violently that he had to sit near the center pole, steadying and reinforcing it with his grip. Before long, likely on the night of 20 July, the strained seams of the tent reached the bursting point. A rip appeared, and the tent was immediately filled with hissing air. Like an overfilled balloon, the tent split apart, extending orange banners across the snow.

The storm which had been battering our 15,000-foot camp for two and a half days reached the peak of its fury on 21 July. The minimum wind speed was in excess of 60 mph, with frequent gusts that approached 100 mph. The walls of our tent were stretched as tight as a drumhead, sending strong shocks pulsating down the center pole. When a change in the screaming tone of the wind signaled the arrival of still another tremendous wind gust, I would grab the center pole to steady it and to dampen some of the shocks it was receiving. During these hours of peril, my high school Spanish came to mind. I entered in my log book: "Hace mucho viento hoy. ¡Mas horrible!" Schlichter would occasionally launch into a rendition of a currently popular song, "We Gotta Get Out Of This Place."

We were living in an arctic hurricane. It was not possible to stand

148   THE STORMS

outside the tents without being flattened by the wind. Breathing while outside was extremely difficult. If a man faced into the wind, he could not exhale. If he turned his back on the wind, a partial vacuum was created in front of his face, pumping out his lungs as though with a pulmotor, thus preventing him from inhaling.

A six-foot journey outside the tent was a major risk, and required a specific plan of action. One man would untie the tunnel door, and hold it closed like the twisted neck of a paper bag, while the second man poised himself to leap outside. When both men were ready, the door was held open, the adventurer crawled out, and the door was reclosed. The door would be held closed until the outside man returned and called to be let in, then quickly opened while the man jumped inside. Finally, the door could be tied shut again. We were sorely tempted to resort to indoor plumbing, but did not.

Heavy snowfall and dense cloud rode the wind on this day, and in our tent we experienced a repeat performance of the continuously discharging electric spark which had probed us on 16 July at the high camp. Wilcox and Schiff's two-man tent was set up at right angles to the wind, thus serving as an excellent snow fence. Large drifts piled up on both sides of the tent, crushing inward. Wilcox dug the tent out a few times, but the wind was piling snow up faster than he could shovel it away. While crawling in or out of the tent, Wilcox had knocked over the pressure cooker full of gasoline. When their stove ran dry, Schiff and Wilcox would have to use Colorado group stoves.

Talking to Eielson that night, Wilcox said that we were waiting for the weather to improve before making another attempt to climb to the high camp. He anticipated that it might take up to eighteen hours to reach Camp VII once the weather broke. Wilcox mentioned that we were experiencing high winds and drifting snow, and that he had been trying to clear the snow away from his tent.

By 22:00, darkness was added to the gloom of snow and wind. Suddenly, above the screaming wind we heard a frantic shout: "Let me in! Let me in!" Could it be someone from the high camp?! We quickly untied the tunnel door, and Schiff dove in, dragging his sleeping bag. "The tent collapsed under the snow," Schiff told us.

"Where's Joe?!" I asked.

"He'll be over in a minute."

Wilcox arrived with his sleeping bag in tow, and crawled into the tent. We now had five men in a tent suited for three. Lewis, Schlichter, and I had been sleeping door-to-door (lengthwise) in the tent, with the tent pole placed off-center so that one man was to the left of the pole and two were to the right. With two more roommates, a change was in order. We relocated the pole, then put our mattresses and sleeping bags in a sidewall-to-sidewall (widthwise) arrangement, with two men on one side of the pole and three on the other side. The tent was only six feet wide even when its walls were not being pushed inward by snowdrifts, and all of the Colorado men were over six feet tall, so we had to sleep with our feet against the snowbanked walls. Lewis was the tallest, and his feet were in a little alcove that had been kicked into the snowbank.

The storm remained at peak intensity all night long and into the morning of the twenty-second. Then the sky started to brighten, but the wind continued unabated. By mid-morning the sky was cloudless, but visibility was still obscured by ground blizzards. Before noon the wind had removed all loose snow, and we could see the blue sky. All day we lay in our sleeping bags, the passage of time marked only by the movement of the sun's disc as seen through the fabric of our tent.

At the very top of the tent, Schlichter and I spotted an inch-long rip in a seam. We said nothing, not wanting to cause unproductive alarm, but we both started planning a course of action in the event our tent should be blown apart. We arrived at the same conclusion: if the tent split, we would cut through the floor with our pocket knives and try to dig straight down into the snow beneath. All day long we watched the rip, and to our great relief it did not grow any larger.

Lewis had started weakening again on the twentieth, and despite prodding by Schlichter and me, he refused to eat on the twenty-first and twenty-second. The rest of us ate candy, nuts, Logan bread, crackers, and anything else that did not require cooking. Due to our cramped conditions since the other tent collapsed, we had neglected to cook food or melt snow for drinking water for a period of twenty-two hours. I packed snow into my plastic water bottle, then partially melted it by keeping the bottle in my sleeping bag.

In the early evening hours the wind started to die down. To my astonishment, Wilcox began talking about moving up to the high camp. Lewis was seriously ill, Schiff and Wilcox were as weak as rag dolls. Schlichter and I, who had not been ill at any time on the expedition, were still healthy. We were still strong, but five days of sitting in a storm-raked camp had not helped us any. It might have been possible for the two of us to return to the high camp, but this would mean leaving Wilcox, Schiff, and Lewis in Camp VI with only a slim chance of survival.

Eielson asked us that night if any of us could return to the high camp if we were air-dropped food and dry sleeping bags. We had food, and our sleeping bags were not wet. But we also had three sick people. Wilcox looked at Schlichter and me as Eielson asked about a return to Camp VII. We shook our heads, "No." Wilcox replied to Eielson: "Not more than one of us would feel like going up." He was implying that he was willing and able to make the ascent. Willing he may have been, but able he most certainly was not. Relaying a question from Wayne Merry, Eielson asked: "Is anyone frostbitten or in trouble?" Wilcox replied no.

We arranged a radio contact for 23:00 that night, when we thought we would be starting down the mountain. Schlichter and I went outside to sort through the cache. "Those guys aren't going to be able to go down the ridge tonight," Schlichter said, referring to the three men in the tent.

"Yeah, I know," I replied. "We'll have to feed 'em up good and let 'em get a night's sleep, then start down in the morning. I hope the weather holds." We cooked up food and drinks, trying to nourish and rehydrate the weakened men and ourselves.

We contacted Eielson again at 23:00. They were reading us weakly, and I told Wilcox to inform them that we had sick men in the party and therefore could not go back to Camp VII. Wilcox radioed: "We are waiting until morning. We have a couple of people hampered, and cannot travel tonight." At Eielson, ranger George Perkins was able to copy only that we were waiting until morning. He asked for a repeat, but Wilcox merely told him: "That's fine. Waiting until morning to leave." An 08:00 radio contact was arranged for the next morning. Perkins asked if there was anything else. Schlichter and I were outside, digging out Wilcox's tent. I asked Wilcox to give me the radio, and he handed it through the door.

The external battery pack was connected to the radio by a length of insulated wire, which had jack-plugs on either end. The connections were poor, so I had to hold the plugs in place in both the battery pack and the radio, while simultaneously holding the radio and the battery pack themselves, and manipulating the press-to-talk button. An octopus would have been more suited to the task. One or the other of the connections was usually loose, so Eielson had difficulty reading my message. I wanted to tell them that we had sick people in the party. Four times I tried to send the message, and four times Eielson could not copy. They asked for Wilcox to repeat the message, since they thought his voice came through the interference better. I was standing outside in the whistling breeze, trying to hold all the component parts of the radio together. Wilcox had been in the tent, with the radio and battery pack resting on his chest.

I could not try to get Wilcox to repeat something he would not admit, namely that there were sick people in camp, including himself. At Eielson, Haber got increasingly irritated as I kept adjusting the battery jacks and trying again. Perkins would calmly repeat the request for Wilcox to give the message, and high on the icy slopes of Mount McKinley, I would heave a sigh, grit my teeth, adjust the battery jacks, and try again. On the fifth attempt the contacts were finally right, and Eielson got my message: "We have three people pretty sick up here." Eielson copied, and I continued: "This is why we could not go up. We have to get these people down." Now they understood. We confirmed the 08:00 radio contact, and signed off.

Schlichter and I moved our gear out of the Colorado group tent, leaving room for the other three men to stretch out and sleep. We finished digging out Wilcox's tent, swept out the inside, and crawled in with our sleeping bags. We talked for a while, about the events that had occurred, and our plans for moving down Karstens Ridge in the morning. Lewis, Schiff, and Wilcox had been slow and weak descending the easy terrain from Camp VII to Camp VI on the seventeenth. Now they were even weaker, and the terrain below us was treacherous.

We talked about the lost men. I said, "You know what they [the Park officials] are going to say? They're going to say, 'That's a big group, bigger than most expeditions. They've got lots of equipment. We don't think anything too serious could have happened to them.' " I was later surprised by how close I had come to a direct quote.

Schlichter later told me that he did not sleep that night, but stayed awake massaging his feet to prevent frostbite. But I was sufficiently warm, and had no trouble going to sleep. Within minutes of lying down, my whole body seemed to spin, as though the tent was on a huge turntable. I heard a rush of loud noise in my ears, like the sounds of heavy city traffic, and I tumbled into a deep sleep.

9

THE DESCENT

We awoke on the morning of the twenty-third to the sound of an insistent voice: "Howard! Paul! Let's get going!" It was Schiff who was calling us, and I was pleasantly surprised to see that he was eager to start the descent. Schlichter and I jammed our sleeping bags into their stuff sacks and crawled outside.

The breeze was intermittent now, with occasional gusts around 30 mph. Only a few wispy clouds blemished the blue sky. The temperature was remarkably mild, somewhere in the mid 20's. The five-day storm had stripped away vast amounts of loose snow, exposing menacing crevasses below and beside our camp. The trail upglacier stood out above the snow around it, like a little garden wall running through a field.

I pulled my Kelty pack out of the snow beside our tent, where I had anchored it with two ice axes and slings. I turned it upside down to empty out a now-solid block of snow that had drifted in under the closed flap. Schiff emerged from the Colorado group's tent, and collapsed at my feet. "Anshel! Are you okay?!" I asked. Schiff got up to a kneeling position, and replied, "Yes, I'm just dizzy."

Schlichter, Schiff, and I proceeded to pack our gear. Wilcox and Lewis remained in the Colorado tent, despite reminders that they had equipment to pack. Lewis finally emerged, but he took a painfully long time to pack his equipment, sitting down to rest numerous times. Wilcox was once again unable to do his own packing, so he remained in our tent while Schlichter and I dug out his tent, folded it up, and packed his pack for him.

I went into the Colorado tent, and found Wilcox sitting round-shouldered, his cold hands curved into grotesque claws. I opened my shirt and warmed Wilcox's hands on my stomach. The warming improved feeling in his hands, but they remained completely immovable from the wrist down, as though paralyzed.

Wilcox went outside to start the difficult task of putting on his crampons, and I proceeded to clean out the inside of the tent. I found the radio in a corner, covered with snow and not in its protective plastic bag. Snow was packed into the microphone-speaker, and had to be blown out. I put the radio into its bag, and slipped it into a pocket of my pack.

As scheduled, we contacted Eielson at 08:00. After arranging for another contact at 11:00, I apprised the rangers of our situation: "Jerry Lewis and Anshel Schiff are very weak. Joe has frostbitten fingers. We don't know how badly, but he can't move 'em anymore." The message was relayed to Merry, and he asked if we would need any assistance. I replied: "Negative, negative. I believe we'll be able to get down to the Muldrow all right."

Eielson asked about our weather conditions. I reported westerly winds gusting at 25 to 30 mph, and a very mild temperature of 25 degrees or above. Then I mentioned that the high camp had light clouds and blowing snow, but Eielson did not copy, and they asked for a repeat. I repeated the message about the high camp, and added: "I'm holding both battery jacks in at the same time, they slip every once in a while and I get poor contact." We signed off, and returned to our preparations for the descent.

Schlichter and I took down the Colorado tent, and Schlichter lashed it to his pack, then we started to put the final touches on the cache. A great deal of Wilcox group food remained, along with much personal gear belonging to the men of Clark's team. We did not disturb this equipment. Weeks later, we thought we should have searched the cache for films, and taken them down with us. But at the time, that would have indicated that we did not expect the owners to arrive later to claim their own property, something we were loath to admit. Using the waterproofed nylon floor of the burned tent, we covered the cache, pinning the corners to the snow with ski poles and wands.

We were ready to start our descent. As we had done on the descent from Camp VII on 17 July, we tied the two ropes together to form a 270-foot rope. I took the lead position so that I could judge the difficult spots before the sick men had to cross them. Thus I could give instructions or cut steps if necessary. Schlichter took the last-man position. He was the only healthy man other than myself, and I hoped he would be able to stop a fall on Karstens Ridge if any of the men below and ahead of him should slip. I put Wilcox behind me, so he might be able to belay me while I chopped steps or set up a belay anchor point. Behind Wilcox, Lewis and Schiff completed our rope team.

Just before 09:00, we started along the trail, going slightly uphill toward the edge of the glacier. This 150-yard stretch led to the top of the traverse across the flank of Browne Tower. On this broad, firm, and gentle section of the trail, Lewis collapsed three times. Each time he stayed down longer, and rose more unsteadily to his feet. When Lewis would fall, Wilcox and Schiff would immediately sit down and slump over on the snow. Schlichter later told me that he thought, "This is it. We might as well go back [to Camp VI] and call in the helicopter." Lewis and Schiff were in a fainting condition, and Wilcox's hands were so numb that he was unable to hold his ice ax properly. Our prospects for descending the ridge were not too bright.

At the end of the gentle section of the trail, where it began the traverse across the slope of Browne Tower, I turned and looked back toward the high camp. The site of the camp was visible, but there were no tents and no people to be seen. My last shreds of hope for our lost companions vanished, and I turned sadly to the task before us.

From the top of the Browne Tower traverse, I studied the fearsome route ahead. The soft, deep snow that we had waded through on our ascent had all been scoured away, leaving a slope with the appearance and consistency of fresh white marble. I took a few steps onto the slope: my crampons couldn't make a scratch. Our packed trail was still on the face, standing out as a wedge of level snow plastered onto the polished slope. I tested the outer edge of the trail with my foot: it crumbled.

I walked back to where the others were waiting. I did not want to cross the slope, for I was sure that Lewis would fall, and it was unlikely that we could stop a fall on that face. I suggested that we return to Camp VI, and descend along the base of the slope, then gain the ridge near Parker Pass at 14,600 feet. Schlichter and Wilcox were against doing this, and pointed out that there were crevasses at the base of the slope, and that we would be crossing unknown terrain. I agreed, and we prepared to start across the flank of Browne Tower.

In order to have a strong belay for Lewis, I had Schiff trade places with Schlichter, putting Schlichter right behind Lewis. I instructed everyone to step only on the uphill edge of the trail, where the packed wedge of trail met the slope. We started across the slope, like walking on a window ledge across the face of a building. Slowly, cautiously, we proceeded, with Lewis belayed from the front by Wilcox and from behind by Schlichter. On two occasions, sections of the trail split off as I put my weight on them, sending chunks of snow skittering down the slope. I was able to keep my balance, and the others stepped across the weak spots.

With admirable determination, Lewis moved across the slope, not slipping or collapsing, calling for no rest stops. A few dozen yards from Parker Pass and the end of the traverse, my right crampon snapped in half. Within a few yards I would be off the hazardous part of the slope, so I called no stop, preferring to clank along for a while like Jacob Marley in his chains.

Just before our 11:00 radio contact time, we reached Parker Pass, at the top of Karstens Ridge. The descent of 400 vertical feet from Camp VI to Parker Pass had taken less than thirty minutes on 13 July, but today it had required two hours to cover the distance, which was less than a half mile. The storm had exposed many large rocks at Parker Pass, and we sought shelter from the wind behind the largest rock. Here we found the remains of an old cotton tent and two or three five-gallon milk cans. The last party of our expedition to leave Camp I at McGonagall Pass had found some of these same milk cans, and had used them to store the food cache for the descent. Also at Parker Pass was an Ovaltine can with the date 1921 on it, indicating that this had been a camp of some early expedition, perhaps the 1932 Lindley-Liek-Strom-Pearson party.

I repaired my crampon with the spare chain that Lewis was carrying, and strapped it back onto my boot. By the time I had completed the repairs, it was 11:00 and time for our radio contact with Eielson. I told Eielson that we had taken two hours to reach 14,600 feet. "Jerry Lewis is extremely fatigued," I said. "We have Dexadrine in our first aid kit. Could you advise?" Perkins consulted with Merry, but not being familiar with either Lewis's condition or the effects of the drug, Merry was able to offer no advice.

During the traverse from 15,000 feet, I had looked upglacier toward Camp VII several times. I reported to Eielson: "I've been looking up at the site of the higher camp all morning. I can't see any tents, or any people. There's no sign of anything." I told Eielson that we would give Lewis Dexadrine and continue down the ridge. We arranged a 14:00 radio contact, and signed off.

Lewis took one Dexadrine pill, an orange tablet whose heart shape was symbolic of its stimulant effect. I gave Lewis the last of my water to wash down the pill, and we started down Karstens Ridge.

At first the going was easy on the broad, gentle ridgetop. Our packed ascent trail was a continuous wall which stood on the very crest of the ridge, as much as three feet above the surrounding snow. The trail had originally been packed down a foot below the general surface of the ridge, therefore at least four feet of snow had been blasted from the ridge by the storm. Dozens of our wands had also been removed, and only three or four remained on the entire ridge. In a few places we found crazy lines of footprints standing over a foot high, where someone had stepped off the trail during the ascent. The footprints were now preserved, looking like a line of tree stumps.

The surface of our old trail was uneven, and too hard for our crampons to penetrate, so we walked beside the trail where some soft snow had drifted up against the wall. Around 14,200 feet, the crest became so narrow that the old trail covered it completely, and we were forced to walk on the trail. It was like walking on an uneven stone wall, with our crampons clinking and scratching as we teetered along the ridgetop. At 14,000 feet, the ridge started its plunge down the steep Coxcomb. Although steep, it was broad again, and it had sufficiently soft snow to afford good purchase for our crampons.

From the Coxcomb, we were able to look down the ridge to the site of Camp V, at 12,100 feet. There was something new in this world of white and black: we could see the orange tents of the Mountaineering Club of Alaska Expedition, in our old campsite. Several climbers could be seen walking in the camp.

We were able to move comparatively easily on the Coxcomb, despite its steepness. Twice I heard "Whoa!" from Schlichter or Schiff, and assumed they were calling rest stops. Both times I stopped immediately, but the rope between Wilcox and me kept slithering down the slope, indicating that Wilcox was still moving downward. Each time, I turned and looked up the slope, and was surprised to see not only Lewis and Schiff, but also Schlichter sprawled out in the snow. After the second time, Schiff shouted, "Damn it, when we yell 'whoa,' stop! Jerry has been falling!"

My heart jumped to my throat. I shouted back, "If someone falls, yell 'falling,' not 'whoa' "! Discussing the incident later, Schlichter recalled, "He wasn't exactly falling. More of a crumple. 'Crumpling!' "

We reached the upper end of our highest fixed line at 13,300 feet. Our black polypropylene fixed line was not the only one on the slope anymore. The storm had uncovered a manila line and a yellow poly line, which paralleled ours down the Coxcomb. Each of us in turn clipped onto our line with a carabiner and sling. Thus protected in case of a slip, we moved quickly down to the lower end of the fixed line at 13,000 feet. Our Coxcomb cache was located here, tucked safely behind a rock.

All five of us gathered at the cache while I dug out the Colorado

Group's three-day food bag. I tied the twenty-four-pound food bag on top of my pack, and we were ready to start down the ridge again. Or nearly ready. Lewis was sitting down, and I asked the usual "Ready, Jerry?" He replied, "No, I can't."

Clouds were moving rapidly down the mountain toward us. The peak was obscured from 14,000 feet upward, and the valleys below us were cloud-filled as well. I said, "Jerry, we've got to get going. The weather's closing in. The camp's just down the ridge, and the Alaska group is there. We've got to get going."

His head hanging wearily, Lewis replied slowly, "You'll just have to leave me behind." Earlier in the day, this kind of talk would have worried me greatly. But here, just 900 vertical feet above an occupied camp, I felt that the situation was pretty well under control. I took Lewis's rope and pulled him gently to his feet. Once again we were underway.

At 12,800 feet we were confronted with a pitch that was not only steep, but as hard as cement. I asked Wilcox to give me a belay while I chopped several steps down the fifteen-foot pitch. We reached the top of the bergschrund wall at 12,700 feet, and clipped in to the fixed line which we had installed there, moving quickly to the lower end of the fixed line at 12,600 feet.

The Alaska group was waiting for us just down the ridge. They had seen us start down the Coxcomb, and knowing that we were a twelve-man expedition, they wondered where the other seven men were. As they had watched us descending the Coxcomb, they had seen Lewis fall down twice, and decided that we were having problems. They brewed up some hot drinks and put them in thermoses, then started up the ridge to meet us.

The Alaskans awaited us at 12,500 feet. Their leader, Bill Babcock, was the first to meet me as I came down the ridge. He was a somewhat shocking sight, wearing ice-coated woolen mitts that were stained with blood from his chapped and cracked nose. Babcock tactfully asked me, "Is everyone all right?"

I replied, "The third man's pretty sick." After giving us all a round of hot Kool-Aid, they took Lewis's full pack and gave him one of their empties, and we started down toward camp at 12,100 feet. The fog became so dense that we could see only one step at a time, and were unable to tell if the ridge was a foot wide or ten yards wide.

We arrived in our old Camp V just in time for our 14:00 radio contact with Eielson. Lewis was hustled into one of the Alaska group's tents, and the rest of us gathered around the radio. The lower altitude had done wonders for Wilcox, and he took charge of the radio once again. Our batteries were weak, and Eielson was unable to read our transmissions, although as usual we were able to read Eielson quite well. Schiff ordered, "Paul, go dig the fresh batteries out of the cache, quick!" This was the first I had known that our spare batteries had been left at Camp V on the ascent.

Haber instructed Wilcox to communicate by clicking the transmitter button, three times for "yes" and twice for "no." He told us to watch Lewis for changes in personality or rationality, signs of lowered body temperature. Haber then determined our approximate location on the ridge by calling off elevations in 500-foot intervals, starting at 14,500 feet, and asking us if we were below that specific elevation.

Haber asked if Wilcox wanted an all-out rescue called, and Wilcox replied with two clicks: "No." We rigged up the dipole antenna, and Eielson was able to understand voice transmissions. Haber asked again if Wilcox wanted an all-out rescue, and Wilcox again said no. Finding this hard to believe, Haber asked a third time, and received his third negative reply. Wilcox continued, "I was asked if I wanted a rescue called at the present time. What can we accomplish if we do this before Sheldon's flight?" Haber replied that it was a matter of getting Wilcox's go-ahead before any rescue could be started.

Wilcox informed Eielson that we were in camp at 12,100 feet, with the MCA Expedition. He concluded with: "I would like a rescue pending Sheldon's flight. From information based on Sheldon's flight should a rescue be decided." After arranging for our usual 20:00 radio contact for that evening, Wilcox signed off. Babcock, who had been surprised by some of the radio conversation, began conferring with Wilcox.

I crawled into the MCA group's Logan tent where Lewis was resting. He was being given luxurious treatment, while reclining on a soft bed. He had warm drinks and Alaskan delicacies such as smoked salmon and moose jerky to please his palate and rebuild his strength. He had heard the radio, which had been just outside the tent. He grinned and said, "Have you noticed any changes in my personality?"

I replied, "You were pretty darn sick, Jerry. You wanted us to leave you at the Coxcomb cache."

One of the members of the Alaskan group, Grace Jansen-Hoeman, was a doctor, and she had discovered that Lewis had minor frostbite on his feet. The frostbite had been brought on by dehydration, undernourishment, and fatigue while we were pinned in at the 15,000-foot camp. Unlike Schlichter, Lewis had fallen asleep during our last night at 15,000 feet. Schlichter had massaged his feet to prevent frostbite, but Lewis had not. The toe of his sleeping bag had been damp from frost and from contact with the snowbanked tent wall. Combined with Lewis's weakened state, these conditions were sufficient to cause the frostbite.

Lewis remained in the Alaska group's tent, and I went out to help Schlichter dig out a tent site and set up our tent. As we were pecking away at the snow with our small aluminum shovel, Babcock walked over with his group's huge aluminum-alloy coal shovel. Using the big shovel we were able to move great heaps of snow very rapidly, and soon had our tent set up and our gear placed inside.

I stood outside and talked briefly with Gayle Neihauser, and then at some length with John Ireton and Chet Hackney of the Alaska group. They asked my opinion about the probable condition of the lost men. I answered indirectly, saying that since we had heard nothing from Clark's team in six days, I could only feel that they were in really serious trouble. I mentioned that no tents were visible at the high camp, another possible indication of trouble.

The MCA group was composed of experienced, well-conditioned Alaskans who had known one another and made climbs together before. Despite this definite advantage, Ireton and Hackney told me that they had experienced problems too. They did not use horses to pack in any of their gear, and had spent two days walking in the soaking rain only to discover they had picked the wrong valley. They had intended to follow Cache Creek to McGonagall Pass, but had mistakenly gone up Carlson Creek instead. Two of their original nine-man party had called it quits, and returned to Wonder Lake. When the expedition reached McGonagall Pass and looked upglacier at the crevasses of the Lower Icefall, another man decided this climb was not for him. He returned to Wonder Lake, making a solo crossing of the treacherous McKinley River.

Ireton had been suffering with debilitating and persistent diarrhea. Kaopectate from the Alaska group's first aid kit had no effect, and Ireton was wondering if he would be able to complete the climb. I dug a bottle of prescription paragoric out of the Colorado group first-aid kit, and gave it to Ireton. He later told me that the medicine did the job, curing his illness completely.

The Alaska group happened to be using the same gasoline stoves as the Wilcox group, the Optimus 111-B. I told them of the troubles the Wilcox men had experienced with the stoves. Ireton said the Alaska group's stoves had been used without incident.

Schlichter and I were in our tent in the early evening, just about to start cooking dinner, when Bill Babcock came to the front door. He had finished his talk with Wilcox, having tried to convince him that an all-out rescue should be called for the seven lost men. Wilcox was not completely recovered from his illness that had affected him from time to time ever since we reached 15,000 feet on 12 July. He still could not bring himself to believe that Clark's team was in mortal danger, just as he had been unable to realize that he, Schiff, and Lewis were dangerously ill at Camp VI. Babcock summed up his thoughts: "Wilcox sounds looney." We discussed the situation, and I told Babcock about the locations and contents of our food caches. He was hoping to climb without equipment relays, in an attempt to reach our high camp as soon as possible.

Babcock left, and his younger brother Jeff came over to spend the night in our tent, since Lewis was staying in an Alaska group tent where the doctor could keep an eye on him. Even a diet of smoked salmon and moose jerky can get old after a while, and Jeff Babcock was glad to sample our Swiss steak dinner.

At 20:30 that evening, we heard an excited shout from Schiff: "There's a full-scale rescue underway! Do you want your parents notified?" Schlichter and I said yes, since we wanted our folks to know that we were not the objects of the search.

Wilcox had nearly finished the radio contact before we knew it was taking place. Babcock had convinced Wilcox that a rescue was necessary. From Eielson, Haber asked for Wilcox's opinion on dispatching a large Air Force rescue plane to make a high-level overflight of the peak. Wilcox replied that he was in favor, and added: "If this means calling this an all-out rescue at this time, this is what we must do."

Without consulting or even informing the Colorado men, Wilcox had agreed to turn our radio over to the Alaska group, a radio which we had paid for on an equal basis with the Wilcox group. The MCA was carrying radios with which they hoped to be able to talk to Fairbanks, but they had been unable to make contact so far on their climb. Our radio was preferable not only because it was proven, but it was also smaller, lighter, and usable for communicating with the rangers at Eielson Visitor Center.

The snowfall and heavy fog that had closed in on us just as we reached 12,100 feet continued all night. By the morning of 24 July, conditions had improved very little. Wilcox made his last radio contact with Eielson that morning. Schlichter and I did not know a radio contact was scheduled, and were therefore not in on the conversation with Eielson. Not knowing that our radio had been given away, we did not realize that this was to be our last contact.

Wilcox asked if he could be airlifted out, so that he could accompany the Air Force reconnaissance flight. At Eielson, Perkins replied no, that there was no plan to pick Wilcox up before he returned to Wonder Lake. Wilcox offered to accompany a rescue team, if he was first allowed to dry out his gear at Wonder Lake. Dr. Jansen-Hoeman was suffering with a migraine headache, and Babcock persuaded her to descend with us, to enable the remaining five men to travel at top speed. Wilcox informed Eielson that Dr. Jansen-Hoeman would be hiking out with us.

Wilcox was starting to grasp the immensity of the situation we had become involved in, and he asked Perkins: "What is Merry's opinion on calling an all-out rescue at the present time?"

Perkins replied: "His personal opinion is that something more should be done than the reconnaissance flight [by Sheldon], particularly considering the bad weather. However, we're having problems here on up the line." Perkins said the decision for an overflight by a large Air Force plane was not a decision Merry could make. Wilcox asked who would make the decision, and Perkins answered: "That's one of the problems here right now. This would come from the Superintendent or the Chief Ranger. The opinion of those who would make it [the decision] is that we should wait on Sheldon."

Wilcox ended his transmission with: "My opinion is that the high-altitude plane should be sent up now, or as soon as possible." Despite several attempts by Eielson to call Wilcox, the radio at Camp V fell silent, perhaps blotted out by heavy interference from other stations, the only such interference we had experienced during the expedition.

We spent a leisurely morning packing our gear for the descent, hoping the fog would thin before we started down. We retrieved our rubber boots from the ascent cache, massaged them until they were soft, and put them on. Lewis gave his expedition down parka and his felt boots to Babcock, for use in case someone was found at the high camp. Babcock instructed Lewis to pick up an identical parka at Babcock's home in Anchorage, in return for his own.

As soon as Lewis emerged from the tent it became apparent that he was quite weak, and his feet were very painful. Dr. Jansen-Hoeman gave Lewis a codeine pill to lessen the pain. Schlichter and I took the heaviest Colorado group gear, leaving only some freeze-dried foods and some aluminum pans for Lewis to carry.

Around noon the wind started to pick up, whipping snow through our camp. By 13:00 we were all roped up and ready to go. Schlichter, Lewis, and I were on one rope, while Wilcox, Dr. Jansen-Hoeman, and Schiff were on another. I waved my ice ax to the men standing in the camp, and we started down.

We had 550 vertical feet of very narrow ridge between us and the relative safety of the saddle at 11,550 feet, where we would leave the ridge. Within minutes of leaving camp, the wind increased, lashing us with blinding snow driven by 35-mph gusts. While our eyes were being blasted with snow, and the ridge was obscured by hissing drifts, we could only stand still and hope we would not be blown off the mountain. Our large packs made us poor examples of aerodynamic design, and I feared that Lewis in his weakened condition might be knocked down by the wind. Lewis had been up this section of the ridge only once, under conditions very similar to those we were faced with now. It was not his favorite part of the mountain.

During one of our forced stops on the ridgetop, the wind hit me strongly on my left side, throwing my weight heavily on my right leg. The snow under my right boot crumbled, and my leg plunged off the ridge. I reflexively straightened my left leg, lifting myself back to the ridgetop. In so doing, one of the crampon spikes on my left boot sliced through my trousers and made a neat incision behind my right knee. I noticed it later, when sweat made the cut sting, and I looked down to see my trouser leg stained with blood.

We continued down the ridge, and I felt greatly relieved when we reached the saddle. I started the traverse down the face of Karstens Ridge, heading for the Muldrow Glacier just 350 vertical feet below us. The snow was exceptionally deep, and I was wading through it at waist depth. Lewis was right behind me, and he needed frequent rest stops. It looked like a repeat of our descent from 15,000 feet was developing. At one point, as I was pushing through the deep snow, the snow around my legs and waist suddenly moved, carrying me about two feet down the slope. It was a potential avalanche, but I was surprised that it did not frighten me. I merely thought to myself as I slid down the slope, "So what else can happen?" We finally reached the valley floor and plodded through foot-deep snow to the site of Camp IV, at 11,000 feet. We had taken two and a half hours from 12,100 feet, the site of Camp V.

We stopped to pick up a Colorado group first-aid kit and some freeze-dried foods from the cache. Wilcox's rope team was going to continue its descent, so Dr. Jansen-Hoeman gave me the codeine pills for Lewis. Schlichter and I took all of the group gear that Lewis was carrying, in order to lighten his load. Lewis began discarding personal equipment, such as a pair of new ski pants, and even the diary he had kept in the form of letters. I walked over and picked up his letter packet, and said, "Here, Jerry. Heft this, and if it's too heavy, I'll carry it for you." He put the letters back into his pack. He could not find his goggles, so he threw away his goggles case. I put it in my pack. Lewis finally got his pack down to about thirty pounds. Schlichter and I were both carrying our heaviest loads of the climb, over a hundred pounds each.

The glacier ahead of us was generally fairly level, and covered with soft snow, so we took off our crampons and put on our snowshoes. We moved out again, and within fifteen minutes had passed Wilcox, who had stopped to change boots. All of our wands on this section had been removed for use higher on the mountain, and the MCA group had removed all of their wands as well. We found our way down the gently sloping glacier and through the maze of the Great Icefall by following the hint of a trail. Not really a difference in level, but a difference in tone and texture marked our old trail. The difference was due to the way in which the trail had been filled with drifting snow.

The extremely heavy load, along with the soft-soled rubber boots, caused the crosspiece on my snowshoe to aggravate an old injury in my left foot. To alleviate the pain, I pushed my foot as far forward as it could go in the snowshoe binding. This made it impossible to use the hinge of the snowshoe, and required the snowshoe to be slid along flat-footed. In spite of this inconvenience, we made rapid progress.

From the Great Icefall, I looked back toward the top of the peak. The welcome sun had begun to shine just as we were approaching the top of the Great Icefall, and the sky had cleared except for a cloud-cap storm on the summit. Four miles away and 5,000 feet above us, we could see Browne Tower. And there on its flank, we saw our little wedge of trail, a string across a snowbank, white among white.

From the slope of the Great Icefall, the site of Camp III was visible. We moved quickly down to the campsite at 8,075 feet, pausing there to eat some nuts, crackers, and candy from the food cache. Wilcox's rope caught up with us again, and we started downglacier. We reached the two right-angle crevasses just below Camp III, and I crossed the first one without incident. My snowshoe broke through the thin covering of the second crevasse, sending me sprawling safely to the other side. I struggled to my feet, no small task with a hundred-pound pack. Lewis and Schlichter avoided the hole I had made, and we continued down the Hill of Cracks and across the flat toward the Lower Icefall.

The fog began to close in on us. By now it was past midnight, and we were walking in nearly total darkness. We paused momentarily to take off our snowshoes at the top of the Lower Icefall, then started across the toes of the avalanche cones at the edge of the glacier. Lewis's feet were extremely painful while we were walking on the side-hill at the edge of the Lower Icefall, and we moved slowly. His face lined with agony, Lewis weakly hummed the words, "A little bitty tear let me down, spoiled my act as a clown." Weeks later, Lewis discovered that serious damage to tendons and ligaments in his feet had caused the pain, and not the minor frostbite.

Wilcox passed us up just before we reached the base of the icefall. There was an avalanche slope near the base of the icefall, below the two hanging glaciers which had been a concern when we first established the route in June. By now, the twenty-fifth of July, the snow had all melted away from the avalanche slope, leaving only large, rounded blocks of ice. We had to descend through this jumble, like walking down a pile of golf balls that were three and four feet in diameter.

At the base of the icefall, we took a water stop at a large meltwater pool. Below the Lower Icefall, the glacier was saturated, and very little snow remained over the ice. We had gone only a few feet down the glacier from the pool when I poked my boot into a covered crevasse, and withdrew it full of water. A few feet farther along, I broke into another crevasse, this time falling on my face. I crawled off the covered crevasse slowly, not by choice, but rather because my pack allowed no other course of action. We put our snowshoes back on, and continued down the glacier following Wilcox's tracks. I started singing silently to myself—the tune was "Asleep in the Deep."

The fog was very dense, and Wilcox's tracks began to weave widely, back and forth across the glacier. We knew that he was absolutely lost. However, there's something about following tracks that makes a person feel less lost than he really is, so we plodded diligently along in Wilcox's tracks. Soon the glacier was completely free of snow, so we removed our snowshoes again. The early morning sun began to thin the fog out ever so slightly, and ahead we spotted the large transverse moraine that we knew to be less than two miles from McGonagall Pass.

We headed for the moraine, and walked along it for a couple hundred yards. The glacier was growing brighter every minute, and we could see the valley walls on either side. Off to our right, in the middle of the glacier, we saw Wilcox's yellow tent. They had decided to camp. Schiff saw us on the moraine, and shouted, "You're as lost as we are!" We waved, and after a few minutes' rest on the dry, sunny moraine, we stepped onto the ice again and headed for McGonagall Pass.

We were still roped up, but we walked together, carrying the coils of the rope in our hands. At 08:30, in the beautiful sunshine, we reached the McGonagall Pass cache, just below the pass itself. For over four hours, we feasted on delicacies from the cache, and rested on the sun-warmed rocks, like lizards in the desert. We repacked all of our gear for lowland travel. Lewis found his "lost" goggles in his shirt pocket, and a sheepish look covered his face as he recalled that he had thrown away the goggles case at 11,000 feet. I took the case out of my pack and handed it to him.

Schlichter and Lewis discarded their snowshoes and crampons. I lashed one pair of each onto my pack, plus my own, as well as discarded slings and ice screws. I took my poncho, sweatshirt, extra shell parka, and lowland cotton clothes out of the cache. Schlichter and I each put a 150-foot rope on our packs, since we had one in the cache as well as the one we had used on the climb. As finally loaded up, my pack was later weighed out at 114 pounds. Schlichter and Lewis slept as I tied up my pack, working very slowly in a heavy mental fog of fatigue.

I changed out of my woolen pants and shirt, into my cotton gear, and was surprised to see that I had a small spare tire around my middle. I had gained about ten pounds on the expedition, the result of huge, palatable, high-calorie meals. Schlichter had held his own or gained a bit. Lewis had lost about twenty pounds. Looking at his shrunken physique, Lewis commented, "I haven't got anything left to hold up my pants."

Schlichter asked if he could go on over the pass and start down to-

ward the upper forks of Cache Creek, where we planned to set up a
camp. I thought I could look after Lewis all right, so Schlichter started
up toward the pass, seventy or so feet above us at an elevation of 5,720
feet. Within a few minutes, Lewis was ready, and we started up to the
pass.

Moments later we stood on the pass, where a month before a young
and eager expedition had pitched Camp I. It seemed strangely quiet
now, austere, even desolate. Lewis began descending the snow gully
on the other side of the pass. We left the world of ice and rock, and
headed for the green valleys below. But our homecoming could not be
complete.

I followed Lewis down the snowslope. I walked past the edge of a
large rock which protruded from the snow, carelessly forgetting that
snowbanks near rocks are often undermined by melting. My right leg
plunged through the thin shelf of snow, and I toppled face down,
driven into the snow by the 114-pound pack on my back. My camera,
in its hard protective case, was hanging on my chest. The impact of
the fall jammed the case up against the lens, bending the rim of the
lens. My right knee had missed crashing down on the rock by about
two inches, narrowly escaping serious injury. Lewis had not heard the
fall, and he kept walking downward. I got to my feet, and soon caught
up with him.

We reached the site of the first equipment cache at 4,400 feet,
where Mercer had unloaded the horses. Here the narrow canyon
opened up into the broad valley of Cache Creek, and we were suddenly engulfed by the sweet aroma of grass. The summer tundra was a
lush carpet of grass, sedges, and moss. The only odors we had known
for a month were those of kerosene, food, goose down, and people. I
inhaled deeply, over and over, each breath a rediscovery. The valley
reawakened our senses: softness for the touch, gentleness of form and
color for the eyes, mild moistness on our skin. The delicious sweet
scent filled our nostrils, and the gossiping brook prattled in our ears.
Even the taste found something to delight in; the flavor of water which
had filtered through the tundra. The valley was complete, an active,
functioning creature. It was alive.

We stopped just above the upper forks of Cache Creek and set up our tent. It was 14:17. We had been descending for more than twenty-five hours, and aside from the few minutes at the McGonagall Pass cache, had had no sleep in more than thirty hours. In one push we had passed five of our ascent camps, covering the entire Muldrow Glacier segment of the route. We had descended 8,000 vertical feet, and walked fifteen miles across difficult terrain with heavy loads, and with a sick climber in the party. We ate an early supper, and commenced some serious sleeping.

During the night I had a dream in which someone was talking to me. The next morning, Schlichter told me that it was no dream. Wilcox, Schiff, and Dr. Jansen-Hoeman had come down the valley, and stopped by our tent to tell us that they were continuing on toward Wonder Lake.

Rain and drizzle had fallen most of the night. Schlichter happened to be in a low corner of the tent, and by morning his sleeping bag was soaked. He wrung it out and put it in its stuff sack. With the down wet and matted, the bag weighed twice as much as normal, but occupied only one-third the normal volume. We packed our loads, and continued down the Cache Creek valley at 09:30.

We bushwhacked through the willow scrub on the valley floor for a while, then ascended the side of the large moraine where Steve Taylor had strayed off during our hike in. Near the crest of the moraine, we rounded a clump of willows and came face to face with two cow moose, not more than twenty feet away. We stared, and they stared, and then they trotted away.

On the top of the moraine we came upon two bull caribou. They ran out to a high point at the end of the moraine, then turned to watch us. From the moraine we could see Clearwater Creek, and beyond it, Turtle Hill. We knew that the McKinley River and Wonder Lake lay hidden behind the ridge of morainal hills. Lewis was anxious to move along, and to get to Wonder Lake. He was afraid that the frostbite had done serious damage to his feet, and would not let me look at his feet before we left camp that morning, fearful that we might find them in ghastly condition. Schlichter and I had to step lively to keep up with Lewis this morning.

When we reached the point where we were to ford Cache Creek, we had to use great caution in wading across. The stream was swollen from the rain which had been falling for days. We climbed up the steep, fifty-foot-high bluff on the far side of the creek, and began our trek across the level tundra toward Clearwater Creek. Level, that is, except for thousands of grassy hillocks the size of basketballs, which made footing less than secure.

By 16:30, we were standing on the edge of the bluff looking down on Clearwater Creek. On a gravel bar beside the creek, a blue plastic tent was pitched. We hiked down and peeked in. Schiff was inside. He told us that they had reached the Clearwater that morning and attempted to cross it. After much difficulty and a thorough soaking, Wilcox had managed to cross the muddy, rain-swollen torrent. Schiff and Dr. Jansen-Hoeman knew that they would not be able to cross the stream. Dr. Jansen-Hoeman told Wilcox to go on to Wonder Lake alone, and have a helicopter sent in to pick up Lewis.

Wilcox had left his pack beside Clearwater Creek, and struck out for Wonder Lake. He headed across the tundra to Turtle Hill, then down the slope to the banks of the McKinley River. The river was exceptionally high, and very dangerous. Wilcox made the hazardous crossing, which required him to swim three channels of the ice-cold, muddy river. The current once pulled his trousers down around his legs, nearly administering the *coup de grâce*.

Exhausted and battered, Wilcox reached the Wonder Lake Ranger Station. A call was put in for a rescue helicopter. The Army and Air Force refused to provide one, so a private helicopter was hired, at $120 an hour. The helicopter was based at Farewell, over 100 miles from Wonder Lake.

At the bank of the Clearwater, we were not too pleased with the situation. Unaware that we had no radio in the group, I wondered why Wilcox had not radioed for a helicopter to be sent in. Lewis was upset that a helicopter had been called in for him, without even consulting him first. He wanted to continue on to Wonder Lake, as did Schlichter and I. We were only seven walking miles and 400 vertical feet from the road at Wonder Lake. Pacing up and down the bank, we looked for a place to cross. We thought we could make it across the stream, but we knew that it would be quite dangerous. We decided to sit and wait, to see if a helicopter would arrive.

Just before 21:30, as it was starting to get dark, we heard the whine and churn of a helicopter. It appeared over the river bluffs, wheeling in a wide arc toward the camp. Lewis unrolled a few feet of toilet paper and held it out to serve as a wind indicator. There was no wind, something the pilot was glad to know. The helicopter landed, and out stepped Wayne Merry and Mr. Gray, the pilot. The helicopter was a three-place craft, but we were told that four people could ride if one sat on another person's lap.

Lewis and Dr. Jansen-Hoeman were to be flown out to Wonder Lake first, and Merry asked if we wanted the helicopter to fly back and pick us up, a matter of less than twenty minutes additional flying time. I was against it, but Schlichter and Schiff were in favor. Schlichter said, "I don't want to have to try and swim that river." Not only was I outvoted, I was also a poorer swimmer than Schlichter. I said to Merry, "I guess I'm the only cheapskate. Send it back for us."

Lewis and Dr. Jansen-Hoeman loaded their gear on the cargo racks above the helicopter's landing skids, and climbed in. With the doctor sitting on Merry's lap, they lifted off, and landed just across the creek to pick up Wilcox's pack. Then they were off again, and the helicopter's blinking red lights disappeared into the night sky over the stream bluffs.

We hurriedly packed our gear, including our tent which we had set up to dry. The helicopter returned, and we loaded our gear while the pilot filled the gas tank from some five-gallon cans. We climbed in, with Schiff taking a seat on my lap. The engine roared, and Clearwater Creek began to fall away beneath us. Within a couple of minutes we were flying over the McKinley River, which glistened in the darkness below like a white snake on black velvet. The braided channels had vanished, the river was filled from bank to bank. It was a mile wide; a cold-water Mississippi. I was suddenly very glad that we were crossing it in a helicopter.

Upon arrival at Wonder Lake, Merry took us into the ranger station and distributed the mail that had been piling up. At least, he distributed the portion he could. He returned the keys, wallets, and film that we had left with him, then ushered us into his living room. His wife served us milk and cookies, while we sat in real chairs. The Colorado men were to spend the night in a house trailer behind the ranger station. As we were leaving the house, Schlichter said to Mr. and Mrs. Merry, "Thanks for the cookies, and the milk, and the light, and the chairs, and the roof." Nothing makes a man more sensitive to everyday comforts than being without them, and we enjoyed becoming reacquainted with "civilization."

Before bedding down, we took showers. The water was cold, but that was unimportant. What was important was that the water was clean, and for the first time in well over a month, so were we.

Early the next morning, the twenty-seventh of July, Lewis and Dr. Jansen-Hoeman were flown out to Farewell by helicopter, and from there to Anchorage in a small Civil Air Patrol plane. Schlichter and I packed up Lewis's truck, and prepared to drive out to Park Headquarters. Before leaving Wonder Lake, we talked with Merry for a while. He asked where we would be in Anchorage, so that we could be contacted and airlifted back onto the peak by helicopter if the need arose for some rescue personnel who were pre-acclimated to the high altitude. We told him that we would be staying with Dr. Jansen-Hoeman. Any flight involving high-altitude turbo helicopters would have to originate in Anchorage, so we would be readily available.

We said goodbye to Merry and to Wilcox, who was staying at Wonder Lake for a while. Schiff wanted to hitch a ride, so the three of us climbed into the truck and started toward the village of McKinley Park, eighty-six miles away. Twenty-one miles from Wonder Lake, we stopped at Eielson Visitor Center. We talked with Gordon Haber and George Perkins, who had been our radio contacts. They played some of the recordings of our radio conversations for us, and said they would make copies for us later.

Rain and fog had prevailed in the Park for about two weeks, and today was no exception. A few days before, heavy rains had caused extensive flood damage along the park road, weakening a concrete-and-steel bridge and washing out a roadfill over a culvert. Travelers had been stranded at Wonder Lake, but today bulldozers had cut fords

across the two streams, bypassing the bridge and the roadfill. The
rangers were going to conduct everyone out at the same time, and
Eielson Visitor Center was the gathering point for the convoy.

When we arrived at Park Headquarters, we went in to talk with
Chief Park Ranger Arthur J. Hayes and Park Superintendent George
A. Hall. I pointed out our route and our campsites on a map in the
office. Hall said that he thought it was possible that Clark's team had
mistakenly gone down the West Buttress side from Denali Pass, and
might be safely dug in at some camp. I replied that confusing the
routes was not very likely, because the West Buttress route drops off
steeply from Denali Pass, whereas the Harper Glacier is nearly level at
the pass. Besides, I asked, if the team was safe, why had no one come
down?

Hall said, "We've checked over their application forms. They've got
some experienced men, including a couple with rescue experience. We
don't see how anything too serious could have happened to a party
that large."

Schiff exploded: "What do you mean, nothing could have happened
to them?! They haven't been heard from in ten days!"

On the mountain, we had begun to worry on the night of the nineteenth. At the base of the mountain, men who understood mountains
and climbing began to worry just slightly later. But in more distant
places, some were still not convinced, because they could not imagine
the irresistible power of a high mountain storm.

That afternoon we left McKinley Park. Schiff boarded a train for
Anchorage. Schlichter and I drove east along the Denali Highway. In
the evening we looked back to the west, where the sky had cleared.
There on the horizon, with the sun gilding its icy robes, loomed
Denali—The Home of the Sun.

10

REFLECTIONS

On 28 July, Camp VII felt the tread of a team of climbers for the first time since Clark's party had left for the summit, eleven days before. The Mountaineering Club of Alaska Expedition had reached the 17,900-foot camp, having climbed from 12,100 feet without equipment relays, relying partly on food caches established by our expedition. On the twenty-seventh they had reached the cache at 16,500 feet, finding the food and snowshoes undisturbed. The next day they continued on toward Camp VII, finding Steve Taylor's ice ax at the top of the upper icefall and his sleeping bag draped around the bamboo pole just downglacier from the camp. At Camp VII they were confronted with a grisly montage of ruin—and death. Steve Taylor's body was in the wind-shredded Logan tent, in a sitting position as though clinging to the tent pole. McLaughlin's homemade Cascade tent was intact, but buried by drifted snow. Gayle Neihauser cut through the roof of the tent and looked inside. The tent was full of snow that had sifted in through the zipper, but there were no people and no sleeping bags.

Schlichter and I had arrived in Anchorage on 28 July, and went to visit Lewis at the hospital. That evening Schlichter, Schiff, and I were at the home of Dr. Jansen-Hoeman. Throughout the day we had been in contact with the Alaska Rescue Group, asking and answering questions, and late in the evening we were notified that the MCA Expedition had reached Camp VII and found Steve Taylor's body. We had long since lost hope for the missing men, but the news nonetheless came as a sickening shock. It answered some questions and raised others. The summit team had not made it back to Camp VII. Where were they?

The MCA Expedition continued their climb on 29 July. John Ireton and Chet Hackney, following directions dropped by glacier pilot Don Sheldon, found two bodies and a wand on the steep, crevasse-scarred slope north of Archdeacons Tower. The descriptions of the clothing worn by the men matched that worn by Luchterhand and Walt Taylor.

In August, Vin Hoeman[4] led an expedition up the West Buttress of Mount McKinley, with the express purpose of looking for any further indications as to what might have happened to the lost summit team. At the site of Camp VII, the expedition found only the ten-foot bamboo pole that was below the camp, its tip by now barely protruding from the snow. They also found three closely spaced wands on the ridge west of Archdeacons Tower, where the summit team must have bivouacked on their ascent. All else had been claimed by the swirling snows, forever to remain in the hall of the mountain king.

The Wilcox-McKinley Expedition was composed of some strong climbers and some weak ones, some with good experience and some with next to none. The group tended to allow the lowest common denominator to determine expedition practice in such matters as equip-

---

[4] Vin Hoeman died on Dhaulagiri in the Himalayas in 1969, swept to his death by an avalanche that also killed four other Americans and two Sherpas. Vin's wife Grace (Dr. Jansen) led an all-woman expedition which climbed Mt. McKinley in 1970. She died in 1971, victim of an Alaskan avalanche.

ment usage and use of time on the trail. One might be inclined to conclude that the Wilcox Expedition was uniquely accident prone, but such a conclusion would be erroneous. The mistakes the group made are the same mistakes made by every expedition to a greater or lesser degree.

Both before *and* since the Wilcox Expedition, other expeditions on Mount McKinley have made mistakes as bad, had personnel as inexperienced, or had accidents. One expedition lost all of its stoves, but continued climbing upward, without water or cooked food for days. An immobilizing storm would have killed them. One group had members no more experienced than Steve Taylor, while another had climbers unequal to the physical demands of the peak. On yet another climb, a pressure cooker exploded inside a tent. In each case, the group involved reached the summit and returned safely.

Even the hypothetical "perfect expedition" can be hit by sudden illness, or swept away by an avalanche. But usually nothing major goes wrong, and the minor mishaps and mistakes which are encountered by every expedition are immediately forgotten when they have no ill consequences. Climbers who reach a summit and return safely despite mishaps or misjudgments are hailed for their heroic perseverance, whereas those who persevere only to be trapped by a worsening turn of events are dismissed as foolhardy. How it alters our viewpoint, that intangible called success.

The Wilcox Expedition had tragically bad luck. But life's hold is much too tenuous in the mountains to trust it to luck. A three-hour delay in the onset of the fog on the evening of 17 July, or a similar delay in the start of the storm on 18 July would have saved the men. However, time and the atmospheric tides wait for no man. Storms do not appear on a schedule to suit men, so men must adjust to suit the storms. For the best chance of gaining a summit and returning safely, an expedition must plan and act in a manner which will enable it to withstand some bad luck.

There were circumstances and actions which contributed to the disaster that befell the Wilcox Expedition. The misfortune will never be forgotten; therefore the contributing factors should be fully understood, so that they may be avoided by future expeditions.

Wilcox had first tried to organize an expedition composed of his own climbing acquaintances, but one by one they withdrew from the group. He had nearly given up the idea of a McKinley climb when Jerry Clark contacted him. Clark's friends formed almost the entire membership of the original nine-man expedition. Wilcox became the leader of men about whom he knew very little, and with whom he had not climbed. None of the men, including Wilcox, had any high-altitude experience beyond that of Mount Rainier (14,410 feet). Several had good ice-climbing experience, but none had extensive winter experience in cold weather or high winds.

Several men in the Wilcox group were more experienced than Wilcox. Clark had extensive experience, and Janes and McLaughlin also had good experience. Wilcox had enough experience to be a member of a strong expedition. Luchterhand, Walt Taylor, and Russell could have been considered qualified only if the expedition leader knew them personally and could vouch for their abilities. Schiff and Steve Taylor had too little experience to have been on the mountain at all. They were originally supposed to go only as high as the head of the Muldrow Glacier, just above 11,000 feet, as members of the "scientific team" which was later eliminated.

Experience forms can be misleading, and it is therefore essential that the leader know all the members of his group well. Despite his experience, Clark was one of the most poorly conditioned climbers in the expedition, while the relatively inexperienced Luchterhand and Walt Taylor were two of the strongest.

Anyone who plans and organizes an expedition to a large mountain does a vast amount of paper work, regardless of the quality of the planning and organization. Since Wilcox's men were from all over the country, he mimeographed newsletters to keep them informed of the expedition's progress. He also sent copies to the Park Service, and having never before been snowed under by such a blizzard of paper, they assumed that Wilcox had done an extraordinary amount of preparation. A large amount, yes, but most expeditions do as much. It was extraordinary only in that it was mimeographed and widely distributed.

The mere intimation of publicity seeking can backfire, as it did in exemplary fashion in this instance. Wilcox's early references to publicity became magnified out of all proportion as they became known, first within the climbing fraternity and eventually among the general public. The bulk of his planning, which had been done with care and deliberation, was forgotten. Speculation even arose to the effect that the lost climbers had taken calculated risks in order to ensure publicity, a completely unfair and incorrect assessment. The men of the second summit team did not intentionally arrange to spend a night in the open, high on McKinley's slopes. They were not touched by ambitions for fame, and even Wilcox was not so concerned with "firsts" as his pre-expedition correspondence had led many people to believe.

Owing to the feeling of "safety in numbers," some of the men in the group harbored a false sense of security, openly stating that a large, well-equipped team could handle any situation. The superabundance of equipment led some men to handle the gear with less care than it deserved. Men who would never have abused their own equipment, or equipment belonging to a small expedition, sometimes became quite casual in their treatment of gear on Mount McKinley. After all, each man had paid only a small portion of the purchase price, and there was plenty of spare equipment if something should be damaged or destroyed. Hence, the ropes were dropped to freeze in tangled knots, and the snowshoes were kicked to pieces. The stoves were overprimed, overpumped, and allowed to burn dry. After use they were sometimes pitched out onto the ice. Equipment maltreatment was a minority practice within the group, but in the course of a month-long climb its cumulative effects became increasingly noticeable. Mountaineering equipment should be treated as though one's life depended upon it— because of course it does.

At four of the seven camps, including the two highest and most exposed, the two-man tents were pitched at right-angles to the prevailing wind. This presented the maximum surface area to the battering of the wind. Even if the tents were not blown down, they were in danger of being crushed under drifting snow. Had they been pitched parallel to the wind direction, with the door opening downwind, the streamlined configuration would have prevented snow from piling up. Igloos or snowcaves should have been constructed at the 15,000- and 17,900-foot camps, as a precaution against tent failure.

Radio communications are a significant part of an expedition. We carried two Lafayette Dyna-Com transceivers, one with five watts of power, the other with three. The radios performed well, but their effectiveness was severely impaired high on the peak due to the lack of fresh batteries, which had been cached at 12,100 feet. It is important to have good communications from the upper part of the mountain; therefore six ounces of batteries would be a load worth carrying to the highest camp. The Park Service required us to carry a radio, but would not allow us to use the Park Service frequency. They used the radio communications largely as a device to determine our location on the peak. Hopefully, the Park Service will be able to provide localized and frequent weather forecasts for future expeditions. During the Wilcox Expedition the forecasts were for Anchorage, and were infrequent at best.

The Wilcox group's food was plentiful, but not very suitable. Chili makes some people ill at sea level, and the Wilcox menus included chili at 17,900 feet. At least one man developed diarrhea, and others were likely weakened by the high-starch, low-protein diet. Wilcox said his menus were checked by a dietician. One might wonder if the dietician worked for a public school system, because the meals were more suited for school children than they were for men engaged in strenuous physical labor at high altitudes.

Wilcox has been criticized by some for not leading the second summit team to the top of the mountain. This is an unjust criticism, because Wilcox was the expedition planner and organizer, not a guide. As in any expedition, we usually had two or even three teams doing separate tasks at the same time. Wilcox could hardly be expected to have been on three teams simultaneously. What is more, Wilcox was ill on 17 July, and would have been a hindrance rather than a help to the summit team. The second summit team was left in the experienced hands of Jerry Clark, who was the deputy leader of the expedition.

The aforementioned factors, regardless of their importance, would have been immediately forgotten if the expedition had been successful. This is because these factors did not lead directly to disaster. But there were a number of occurrences and decisions that did lead to the incidents of 17 through 20 July. First was the lack of wands in Camp

VII on the first summit day, which resulted in the route being poorly marked.

The leader must always direct his party with an eye to the multitude of dangers which are lurking on the horizon. Decisions must be made on the basis of good judgment and knowledge of capabilities and obstacles, rather than on the basis of sentiment, aspirations, or expediency. The decisions were theoretically in the hands of Jerry Clark. However, expedition leaders are rarely dictators, and Clark certainly was not. Decisions are generally reached through consensus, wherein experience, ambition, prudence, and enthusiasm all present their points of view. Aside from the intra-party pressures Clark became subject to, there were two other extremely important factors which influenced the decision-making process. These were the altitude, with its slow-down effect on both mind and body; and the overpowering desire to reach a difficult goal that was so very near, a desire which pushes men far beyond their capabilities. It is when compelled by such consuming desire that men tread the razor's edge between superhuman achievement and spectacular failure.

Beginning on 15 July, a series of decisions was made that led directly to the loss of the summit team. The first decision was that of spending the day of 15 July in Camp VII instead of going to the summit with the first summit team. Clark knew full well that the team at 15,000 feet had four of the least experienced men in the expedition, and this may have been one of several factors which prompted him to postpone his summit attempt.

The days of good weather which we had experienced on Karstens Ridge and the Harper Glacier, coupled with the first team's "easy" climb, may have lulled the second team into a lack of respect for the dangers of the upper mountain. Clark's summit team left the high camp in the mid-afternoon of 17 July, having allowed at least three hours of perfect weather to slip by. They took sick men, and set a slow pace. Anticipating their slow pace, they carried sleeping bags in case of a bivouac. A start three hours earlier would have put them on the Archdeacons Tower ridge at 19,550 feet before the fog closed in. They would have been able to see the route ahead, and would likely have made the summit without a bivouac.

As they had ascended the ridge above Denali Pass, the climbers had certainly observed the signs of the weather which was approaching them. They were either unable to comprehend what these signs meant, or they believed that they could force their way through a storm. Finding themselves fogged in on the night of 17 July, the men decided to spend the night in the open, and continue to the summit in the morning. They had likely not wanded their ascent route, and perhaps they thought it would be too difficult to follow on a night descent. On the morning of the eighteenth, with Russell too ill to continue, the team nonetheless decided not to return immediately to Camp VII, but rather to go on to the summit. This was their last chance, the last intersection with the road to survival.

We must hope that something worthwhile has been learned from the Wilcox-McKinley Expedition. This experience, gained at such a fearful cost, should help safeguard future expeditions on Mount Mc-Kinley and elsewhere. If not, our lost friends have surely died in vain.

"One cannot conceive grander burial than that which lofty mountains bend and crack and shatter to make, or a nobler tomb than the great upper basin of Denali."

—Archdeacon Hudson Stuck,
   The Ascent of Denali, 1914

APPENDIX 1

Glossary

avalanche cone—a steep, fan-shaped deposit of snow which accumulates at the base of an avalanche slope.

belay—n: an anchor for securing a climbing rope. vb: to protect a climber against a fall by tending and securing his rope, as by looping the rope around an ice ax which is pushed into the snow.

bergschrund—the uppermost crevasse on a mountain glacier. It separates the moving glacier from the relatively immobile ice adhering to the wall of the mountain.

bivouac—n: an impromptu camp, often in the open without shelter. vb: to make such an encampment.

braided stream—a stream flowing in several dividing and reuniting channels, the division being due to the blocking of channels by deposited sediments.

carabiner—a metal snap link, used to attach ropes to slings, ice screws, and ice axes.

cornice—an overhanging shelf of snow, formed on the downwind side of a ridge.

couloir—a mountain gully, especially a snow-filled gully.

crampon—n: a metal frame with ten to fourteen spikes which is strapped onto a boot to afford traction on ice and hard snow. Used in pairs. vb: to climb using crampons.

crevasse—a crack in a glacier, caused by differential rates of flow within the glacier, especially where the glacier flows over an irregularity in the land surface.

fixed line—light rope which is strung along particularly steep or difficult sections of a climbing route, when the route is to be crossed several times.

ice ax—a specially designed, lightweight ax, with a pick and an adze on its head. For use as a belay point, a handhold, and for chopping steps in ice or hard snow.

ice screw—an auger-like screw, with a ring at the end for attaching a carabiner. Used as an anchor point in ice.

icefall—a portion of a glacier with many crevasses, occurring where the glacier flows down a steep gradient.

kettle—a depression created when a buried glacial ice block melts. When filled with water, it is called a kettle lake.

moraine—a mound, often ridgelike, of unsorted rock debris deposited by a glacier.

ogives—a series of transverse swells and swales on the surface of a glacier below an icefall.

picket—a tubular aluminum pole used to anchor a fixed line.

prussik—n: a special type of knot that holds fast under tension, but slips easily when tension is released. vb: to ascend or descend by use of prussik slings on a climbing rope.

rope—n: the climbing rope, also the team of men tied together on one rope. vb: to tie in to a climbing rope.

sastrugi—wavelike snow forms with a sharp prow pointing into the wind.

serac—an ice tower, usually resulting from the intersection of two or more sets of crevasses.

sling—an auxiliary loop of rope.

traverse—n: a horizontal or diagonal crossing of a mountain slope. vb: to make such a crossing.

tundra—treeless arctic or alpine areas characterized by a vegetative cover of mosses, sedges, and grasses, and generally underlain by permanently frozen subsoil.

wand—n: a stick, usually with a brightly colored flag, used to mark a route on a glacier. vb: to mark a route with wands.

whiteout—a surface weather condition of extremely diffuse lighting, where there are no shadows and the horizon is not discernible. Caused by heavy fog and/or snowfall.

APPENDIX 2

Distance Table

	DISTANCE BETWEEN POINTS	ELEVATION INTERVAL	ELEVATION DIFFERENCE
Highway–Camp I	18 miles	2,000′–5,720′	3,720 feet
Camp I–Camp II	4.5 miles	°5,720′–6,500′	780 feet
Camp II–Camp III	3.5 miles	6,500′–8,075′	1,575 feet
Camp III–Camp IV	3.5 miles	8,075′–11,000′	2,925 feet
Camp IV–Camp V	1 mile	11,000′–12,100′	1,100 feet
Camp V–Camp VI	1.5 miles	12,100′–15,000′	2,900 feet
Camp VI–Camp VII	2.5 miles	15,000′–17,900′	2,900 feet
Camp VII–Summit	2 miles	17,900′–20,320′	2,420 feet
	36.5 miles		18,320 feet

Total distance traveled on foot = 122.5 miles (Snyder, 22 June–26 July)

Total distance traveled on snowshoes = 51.5 miles (Snyder, 25 June–25 July)

° (Note: Camp I was located on McGonagall Pass, 70 feet above the edge of the Muldrow Glacier. The glacier trip from Camp I to Camp II therefore entailed an elevation gain of 850 feet.)

APPENDIX 3

Rope Teams

*—Personnel listed in actual roped order
L—Rope Leader
X—Advance Team (routefinding)
Roman numerals refer to camps (e.g. Camp I)

DATE	ORDER	PERSONNEL	FROM—TO	ADVANCE TEAM
24 June		Clark-L, W. Taylor, Luchterhand, Russell	I–II & return	
25 June	*	Snyder-L, Lewis, W. Taylor, Schlichter	I–II & return	X
		Clark-L, McLaughlin, Russell, Janes	I–II & return	
		Wilcox-L, Luchterhand, Schiff, S. Taylor	I–II & return	
26 June		Snyder-L, Lewis, Russell, W. Taylor	I–II	
		Clark-L, S. Taylor, McLaughlin, Schiff	I–II	
		Clark-L, Schiff	II–I	
		W. Taylor, Russell	II–I	

Date		Team	Route	
27 June	•	Snyder-L, Lewis, S. Taylor, McLaughlin	II–7,300' & return	X
	•	Wilcox-L, Luchterhand, Janes, Russell	I–II	
	•	W. Taylor-L, Schlichter, Schiff, Clark	I–II	
28 June	•	Wilcox, Janes, Russell, Luchterhand-L?	II–III & return	X
	•	Snyder-L, Schlichter, Clark, W. Taylor	short re-routing trip above Camp II	
28–29 June	•	Clark-L, Schiff, S. Taylor, W. Taylor	II–III & return	
		Snyder-L, McLaughlin, Lewis, Schlichter	II–III & return	
30 June–1 July	•	Wilcox-L, Clark, Janes, Schiff	II–III	
	•	Luchterhand-L, Russell, W. Taylor, S. Taylor	II–III & return	
	•	Snyder-L, Schlichter, Lewis, McLaughlin	II–III	
	•	Snyder-L, Clark, Lewis, McLaughlin	III–II	
2 July	•	Wilcox-L, Schlichter, Schiff, Janes	III–10,600' & return	X
	•	Snyder-L, Lewis, McLaughlin, Clark	II–III	
	•	W. Taylor-L, Russell, S. Taylor, Luchterhand	II–III	

DATE	ORDER	PERSONNEL	FROM–TO	ADVANCE TEAM
2–3 July		Snyder-L, Lewis, McLaughlin, Clark	III–II	
		Luchterhand-L, W. Taylor, Russell, S. Taylor	III–II	
		Russell, Luchterhand, Lewis, W. Taylor	II–III	
	*	Snyder-L, Clark, McLaughlin, S. Taylor	II–III	
3 July		Wilcox-L, Schlichter, Schiff, Janes	III–10,600' & return	
4 July	*	Luchterhand-L, Clark, McLaughlin, S. Taylor	III–IV & return	
	*	Janes-L, Schlichter, Schiff, Lewis	III–IV & return	X
	*	Wilcox-L, Snyder, W. Taylor, Russell	III–IV	
5 July	*	Wilcox-L, Russell-L, Snyder, W. Taylor-L (Russell took lead at 11,300', Taylor at 11,500')	IV–11,550' & return	X
		Luchterhand-L, Schlichter, Lewis, Janes	III–IV & return	
		Clark-L, McLaughlin, Schiff, S. Taylor	III–IV & return	
6 July	*	Wilcox-L, Russell, W. Taylor, Snyder	IV–V & return to 11,550'	X
	*	W. Taylor-L, Russell, Wilcox, Snyder	11,550'–V & return to IV	
		Luchterhand-L, Schlichter, Lewis, Janes	III–IV	
		Clark-L, McLaughlin, Schiff, S. Taylor	III–IV	

Date		Rope team	Route / Elevation	
7 July		Wilcox-L, Janes, Luchterhand, McLaughlin	IV–V	
	•	Clark-L, Snyder, Schiff	IV–V & return	X
		Russell, Schlichter, S. Taylor, W. Taylor	IV–10,600' & return,	
		(Lewis in Camp IV, snowblindness)	IV–V & return	
9 July		Wilcox-L, Janes, Luchterhand, McLaughlin	V–12,300' & return	X
		Russell-L, Snyder, Lewis, Schlichter	IV–V	
		Clark-L, S. Taylor, Schiff, W. Taylor	IV–V & return, IV–V	
10 July	•	Luchterhand-L, Schlichter-L, McLaughlin, Janes	V–13,200' & return	X
		(Schlichter took lead at 12,900')		
10–11 July	•	Wilcox-L, S. Taylor, Schiff, Clark-L	V–13,000' & return	X
		(Rope switched end for end during climb)		
	•	Russell-L, Snyder, Lewis, W. Taylor	V–14,500' & return	X
11–12 July	•	Luchterhand-L, McLaughlin, Schlichter, Janes	V–VI & return	
	•	Wilcox-L, Clark, Schiff, S. Taylor	V–VI	
	•	W. Taylor-L, Russell, Snyder, Lewis	V–VI	
12–13 July	•	Luchterhand, Janes, Schlichter, McLaughlin	V–VI	

DATE	ORDER	PERSONNEL	FROM–TO	ADVANCE TEAM
13 July	*	Snyder-L, Schiff, Clark, Wilcox	VI–14,500' & return	
	*	W. Taylor-L, S. Taylor, Lewis, Russell	VI–V & return	
	*	Wilcox-L, Clark-L, Schiff, Snyder (Clark took lead at 15,900')	VI–16,500' & return	X
14 July	*	Snyder-L, Lewis, Schlichter, Clark	VI–VII	
	*	Wilcox-L, McLaughlin, Luchterhand, Janes	VI–VII	X
15 July	*	Snyder-L, Lewis, Schlichter, Wilcox	VII–summit & return	
	*	W. Taylor-L, Schiff, S. Taylor, Russell	VI–VII	X
17 July	*	Snyder-L, Schlichter, Lewis, Schiff, Wilcox (The composition of the second summit team's ropes is conjectural)	VII–VI	
		W. Taylor-L, Russell, Luchterhand	VII–19,550'	
		McLaughlin-L?, Clark, Janes (S. Taylor in Camp VII, altitude sickness)	VII–19,550'	
18 July		W. Taylor-L, Luchterhand (Russell left on trail, likely at 19,550' bivouac site. Altitude sickness)	19,550'–summit & return	

Date		Rope Team	Route/Elevation
		McLaughlin-L?, Clark, Janes	19,550'–summit & descent to approx. 19,400'
		W. Taylor-L, Russell, Luchterhand	19,550'–approx. 19,400'
20 July	*	Wilcox-L, Schlichter, Snyder	VI–15,300' & return
23 July	*	Snyder-L, Wilcox, Lewis, Schiff, Schlichter (Schlichter and Schiff exchanged places after the first fifty yards out of Camp VI)	VI–V
24–25 July	*	Snyder-L, Lewis, Schlichter	V–I
	*	Wilcox-L, Dr. Jansen-Hoeman, Schiff	V–I

APPENDIX 4

Colorado Group Equipment List and Evaluation

E—Excellent, recommended without reservation or modification
G—Good, recommended with minor reservation or modification
F—Fair, recommended only with major reservation or modification
P—Poor, not recommended
U—Unused, not evaluated

PERSONAL EQUIPMENT

Clothing—Low Altitude (below McGonagall Pass, tundra travel)

lightweight cotton shirt, long
    sleeves—E
mosquito head net, army—E
arctic shell wind pants, cotton,
    army—E
rubber boots, foam insulated—G
rubber socks, foam insulated—G

poncho, neoprene coated nylon—E
short pants, cotton—E
1 pr. underpants
1 pr. cotton sweatsocks
1 pr. nylon sweatsocks

Clothing—High Altitude (above McGonagall Pass, glacier travel)

ski pants, non-stretch gabardine—E
wool shirt—E
pullover shell parka, Reevair—G
rubber boots, foam insulated—G
rubber socks, foam insulated—G
spare boot laces

down parka, with attached down-
    filled hood—E
down pants—G
down shirt—E
down underpants, long—U
down booties—E

anklets, waterproof nylon—E
felt boots, army—E
felt "Finn sock" insulation for over-
    boots—E
overboots, nylon—E
6 pr. heavy woolen socks—E
2 pr. silk socks—F
sun hat w. neck flap—E
sun mittens—U

down mittens w. keeper strings—E
gloves, thick raw silk—E
ski mittens, leather—E
2 net undershirts, shortsleeve—E
1 pr. net underpants, long—P
3 pr. underpants, short
stocking cap/face mask—E
goggles, Swiss Everest—G
goggles, army-air force—U
face mask, "surgeons" type—U

Climbing Equipment

ice ax—E
adjustable crampons—F
plastic snowshoes—E
1 ski pole, army—E
3 ice screws—E

waist sling, 1" nylon web—E
4 carabiners, one w. locking gate—E
100' orange avalanche cord—U
rescue pulley—E
3 prussik slings, ¼" nylon—E

Camping and Miscellaneous Equipment

down sleeping bag—E
foam mattress, 3/4 length, 1½"
    thick—G
air mattress, 3/4 length, rubberized
    nylon—E
frame pack, Kelty—E
rucksack, Gerry—E
pocket knife, Swiss—E
fork & spoon set, aluminum—E
plate/dish, aluminum—E
1 qt. canteen, Tupperware—E
plastic cup—E
pocket logbook
large logbook
3 mechanical pencils, 1 wooden
    pencil
map, edited by Washburn—E
lipsalve, Chapstick—E
lipsalve, A-Fil Sunstick—E
signal devices
    mirror, army—U
    flare, flame/smoke—E
    whistle, plastic
compass—U

thermometer w. metal case—E
photographic equipment
    Retina III-S, 35mm—E
    Retina I-A, 35mm—E
    12 rolls, 36 exposure Kodachrome
        II film—E
    unipod attachment for ice ax—E
    lens brush
wristwatch
sunburn cream, Skolex—E
sunburn cream, Sea & Ski—E
toothpaste & toothbrush
playing cards
candle lantern, 2 candles—U
mosquito repellent, Cutter—F
mosquito repellent, Off!—E
stuff sacks for down gear—E
plastic bags for clothing cached at
    McGonagall Pass—E
nail clipper
soap, mercury—E
soap, regular
matches in waterproof case

GROUP EQUIPMENT (3 MAN)

90 man-days of food (see food appendix)

two 150' x 3/8" nylon climbing ropes—E

spare ice ax

325 flagged wands

expedition tent—E

cooking equipment

  2 Optimus 96-L kerosene stoves —E

  Skyline pressure cooker w. spare parts—E

  1½ gal. collapsible plastic water jug

  1½ qt. aluminum pot—E

  2½ qt. aluminum pot—E

  Teflon baking pan (used as skillet)—E

  Nylon spoon

  Pot gripper—E

  Asbestos hot plate (stove platform)

5 gallons kerosene

3 pints alcohol (stove primer)

plastic fuel cans, 1 two-gallon, 2 one-gallon—P

fuel tins, 4 one-liter, 2 half-liter—E

melt tarp

1 roll paper towels—E

4 rolls toilet paper

small snowshovel, aluminum—F

folding saw, for snow—U

whisk broom

2 repair kits, each containing:

  pliers

  rubber patch kit (for boots and air mattresses)

  screwdriver

  wire

  rawhide laces

2 first aid kits, each consisting of: . . . .

Tupperware bread box (to hold first aid supplies)—E

Dexadrine stimulant

Demerol pain killer

Benadryl antihistamine

Pen VK penicillin

Lanoxin digitalis

Seconal sleeping pills

Zincfrin eye solution

Bradosol throat lozenges

burn ointment

zinc oxide

merthiolate

hand lotion (Chapans)

Hinkle pills, laxative

Parapectolin, paragoric

dental floss

talcum powder

milk of magnesia

Isodine gargle

Desenex athlete's foot ointment

adhesive tape

2 Ace bandages, 3" width

salt tablets

aspirin

butterfly closures (for open wounds)

adhesive bandages, assorted

gauze bandage, roll

gauze pads, assorted

mountaineering first aid manual

scissors

tweezers

needle

razor blade

2 sewing kits, each containing: ....

nylon thread, red, white, blue   *12 needles, crewel (large eye)*
carpet thread   *6 straight pins*
waterproof nylon patching material *12 safety pins, assorted*
6 buttons, assorted   *darning yarn*
thimble

GROUP EQUIPMENT (12 MAN)

15 aluminum pickets
1200 feet of polypropylene water-ski tow rope (for use as fixed line)
2 Dynacom transmitter-receivers, 1 five-watt, 1 three-watt

RECOMMENDED ADDITIONAL GROUP EQUIPMENT

"coolie hat" tent anchors
sponge (for bailing out tent)
large aluminum-alloy coal shovel

Comments on Selected Items of Equipment

Some additional observations on selected items which were rated excellent, and all items which were rated good, fair, or poor.

Excellent:

Alp Sport Winter Expedition Tent—a very solid and well-designed pyramid tent, with heavy-duty waterproof floor and waterproof lower sidewalls. Equipped with vestibule extension for equipment storage. Vestibule separated from rest of tent by a zipper door. One large tunnel door at front of tent, two small tunnel doors at rear, in vestibule. Weight, including center pole, eight pounds. This tent was the only one on the expedition that was not crushed, blown apart, or filled with snow during the five-day storm.

Excellent:

Eddie Bauer Down Clothing and Sleeping Bags—superb in comfort and workmanship. Mittens were the finest we had seen, but could be improved by use of nylon outer shell, since cotton mildews if stored while damp. Shirt was wonderfully versatile and comfortable. Sleeping bag was warm and roomy.

Excellent:

Snowtread Plastic Snowshoes—lightweight, compact, durable. Very simple bindings, easy to manipulate with mittened hands. Sunk rather far into deep new snow, but this was expected as a natural consequence of their small size. Supported loads up to 290 pounds, used over rocky moraines and bare ice. Developed some cracks after about thirty miles of use, but these had no adverse effect on the functioning of the snowshoes. The Wilcox group, using identical snowshoes, experienced some difficulty with torn hinges on the shoes.

Excellent:

High Altitude Footgear—combination of wool socks, down booties, felt boots, felt overboot insulation, and nylon overboots. No waterproof or airtight layers. Allowed all perspiration to pass through the layers of insulation as vapor, keeping feet dry and warm.

Excellent:

Tupperware—one quart canisters with pour-spout lids, used as canteens. Fit into side pocket of Kelty pack, did not leak or crack. Entire top could be removed for easy filling, or for packing snow into canteen. Bread box, used as first aid kit. Unbreakable box with waterproof seal, needed a length of cord tied around it to ensure that the lid was not forced off.

Excellent:

Optimus 96–L Kerosene Stoves—easy to operate, compact, efficient, durable. Had to be primed with alcohol, but this became very quick and easy after a little practice. Excepting 15 and 16 July, stoves were used every day from 23 June through 26 July. Fuel use was extremely economical: one and one-eighth gallons of kerosene used or spilled; less than a half pint of alcohol used or spilled.

Excellent (in proper combination):

Air Matresses and Foam Pads—Jerry Lewis used a full-length, nylon-covered, $1\frac{1}{2}''$-thick foam pad in conjunction with a full-length, $\frac{3}{8}''$-thick closed-cell foam pad. Paul Schlichter and I used three-quarter-length air mattresses in conjunction with cloth-covered, three-quarter-length, $1\frac{1}{2}$"-thick foam pads. Judging from our experience, the ideal combination appears to be a three-quarter-length air mattress on the bottom (to keep the person and his sleeping bag away from the wet floor); with a full-length, $\frac{3}{8}$"-thick, closed-cell foam pad on top (to insulate the sleeper from cold convection currents inside his air mattress, and to keep the lower one-fourth of the bag from becoming soiled or wet through contact with the tent floor). The air mattress should not be left fully inflated on a warm, sunny day, or it may explode due to the warming and expansion of the air. The lower one-quarter of the foam pad can be elevated and insulated by placing boots, ropes, and extra clothing beneath it.

Good:

Eddie Bauer Karakoram Down Pants—would have been rated excellent except for one minor difficulty—they were too warm on part of our summit climb, and we could not remove them without removing our boots. This can easily be fixed by installing zippers extending from ankle to knee along the leg seams. Thus modified, the pants could be put on or taken off even while the climber was wearing crampons.

Good:

Red Ball Oneida Rubber Boots and Solar Socks—we used rubber-lined boots, so that the lining would not hold moisture. Unfortunately, a chemical in the Solar Socks which kept them pliable also attacked the rubber lining of the boots, making it gummy and weak. This could be corrected simply by using cloth-lined Oneidas (which are available) instead of rubber-lined Oneidas. High boot socks should be worn with rubber boots, to prevent the tops of the boots from cutting into the wearer's calves. The rubber socks proved very useful as camp slippers, though they were definitely lacking in traction.

Good:

Eddie Bauer Alpine Parka (Reevair coated shell parka)—excellent as a plain shell parka, but the supposedly waterproof-yet-breatheable coating did not work. Body moisture sometimes condensed on the inside of the parka, while rain seeped through almost unhindered. The coating soon began to peel off.

Good:

Swiss Everest Goggles—tended to fog up when the removable side flaps were in place, and provided little protection against wind when the flaps were removed. The flaps were hard to put into place once they got cold and stiff while on the trail.

Fair:

Salewa Adjustable Crampons, Avcin Model—after numerous modifications, these crampons worked quite well. But we experienced too much difficulty in adjusting them to size, and too much breakage on the trail. Breakage can be prevented by bending the ends of the sliding length-adjustment bars so they cannot pull out, and by bolting the extension chain in place; or by replacing sliding bars and chains with chain loops or nylon cord loops.

Fair:

French Aluminum Snowshovel—too small to be very efficient. Developed cracks late in climb.

Fair:

Wigwam Mills Silk Solar Socks—the Norwegian style socks made by Wigwam were excellent, but the silk socks did not perform too well. They worked their way down the wearer's feet, ending up in soft, warm wads at the toes of the boots.

Fair:

Cutter Mosquito Repellent—worked only fairly well just after application, and not at all after the wearer had perspired or waded a stream. By contrast, Off! was very effective and long lasting.

Poor:

Duofold Norse Net Long Underpants—Duofold's net undershirts were excellent, but the net underpants fit poorly and contributed very little to either warmth or comfort. A net undershirt allows perspiration to evaporate without soaking clothing, and the dead air space provides additional warmth. The same principle does not apply with long net underpants, since there is no close-fitting layer on top of them, and therefore no dead air space. A possible solution would be to wear regular long underpants over the net underpants. I no longer use ankle-length net underpants, preferring cotton "thermal-knit" underpants or Duofold's original two-layer underpants. However, I still use and highly recommend net undershirts.

Poor:

Plastic Fuel Cans—these "leakproof" fuel cans leaked badly. I recommend metal fuel cans. We found a one-gallon metal fuel can at McGonagall Pass and carried it all the way to Camp VII at 17,900 feet. The can was the type with a snap-cap vent, and neither the spout nor the vent leaked at any time.

APPENDIX 5

Food

While compiling menus for our expedition, I noticed that previous expeditions' food sounded like survival rations. We wanted food that was good tasting as well as nutritious, and spent months testing various types and brands of food items. Our final menus were not only the most palatable we had heard of, but the lightest in weight as well.

Our food was pre-measured and packed in plastic bags, supper in one bag and breakfast and lunch in another. These two bags were then placed in a larger plastic bag. A one-day food bag contained the food and cooking supplies needed for three men, including a pack of matches and a sponge-backed steel wool pot scrubber. Three one-day food bags were wrapped in a large plastic bag, and bound with masking tape. We had ninety man-days of food, packed in thirty one-day packages which were in turn packed in ten three-day bags. One of the ten large bags became soaked in the rains at McGonagall Pass, causing some soggy lunches and giving rise to fears that much of our food might have been likewise damaged. But no other bags had leaked. We had sealed the meal bags and the one-day bags by wrapping a tight turn of masking tape around the twisted necks of the bags. A better procedure is to heat seal the bags. The three-day bags should have been heat sealed and then bound with fiber-glass reinforced packing tape.

A few of our food items (cheese, slab bacon, butter, honey, jelly) did not lend themselves to pre-packaging, and were therefore carried separately in a "general bag." Had these items been lost or left behind by mistake, it would have had no effect on our self-contained, man-day packaged foods.

The pre-packaged foods weighed 2.67 pounds per man-day. Including the general bag, our food and food packaging weighed a grand total of 3.31 pounds per man-day. Our entire ninety man-days of food, including packaging materials, weighed 298 pounds.

The Armour Star Starlite freeze-dried foods were excellent. For example, the pork chops were absolutely waste free, with no bone or fat. The meat was as mild and greaseless as veal or chicken. Unfortunately, Armour has discontinued Starlite foods, but comparable products are available in other brands. We doubled the manufacturer's suggested one-man portions, except in the case of the beef stew, which we supplemented with sliced beef and gravy, and Rice-a-Roni.

We felt that our lunches were too small, and should have been supplemented with additional dried fruit and baked goods.

Our meals included large quantites of fluids, since dehydration can be a serious problem at high altitudes.

The following is a list of the foods which made up our menus. Quantities stated are individual portions for one day, unless otherwise indicated.

Breakfast
    Cereal—with ½ cup milk; ½ cup Familia, *or* ¼ cup Grape Nuts, *or* 1 single-serving package of Quaker Oatmeal, *or* ¼ cup Ralston, *or* 1 single-serving package of Cream of Wheat
    Meat—scrambled eggs with diced ham, *or* fried bacon
    Beverage—1 qt. orange drink, *and* 1 cup Ovaltine or 2 cups tea
    Dried Fruit—every third day; ⅓ cup prunes, *or* ⅓ cup apricots
    Baked Goods—Logan bread (3″ × 2″ × 1″), *or* 1 small package Ry-Krisp, *or* 6 Triscuits

Jelly—1 tube for three-man group every 3 days, 10 tubes total (strawberry, apple, raspberry, plum, grape, or peach)

Butter—1 can for three-man group every 6 days, 5 cans total

Honey—1 plastic bottle (10 oz.) per man every 6 days, 5 bottles per man total

Lunch

Baked Goods—as above in Breakfast, *or* 4 Fig Newtons

Meat—1 "hickory stick" summer sausage, *or* 1 small can deviled ham

Cheese—edam *or* gouda

Candy—1 bar, Snickers, *or* Milky Way, *or* Forever Yours, *or* Mars Almond, *or* Cadbury Dairy Milk, *or* Payday, *or* Oh Henry, *or* MacIntosh Toffee, *or* Neilson Peppermint Roll

Beverage—1 qt. Wylers drink mix (lemon, orange, cherry, raspberry, or grape)

Sour Fruit Candies—1 assorted flavors roll

Dried Fruit—½ cup; raisins, *or* apricots, *or* prunes, *or* peaches

Nuts—¼ cup; pecans, *or* almonds, *or* black walnuts, *or* cashews, *or* peanuts, *or* Cornuts, *or* English walnuts

Supper

Main Course—pork chops, with fried potatoes and applesauce; *or* Swiss steak with gravy, mashed potatoes, and peas; *or* vegetable beef stew, with sliced beef and gravy, and Rice-a-Roni

Soup—⅓ package, chicken noodle with added chicken bouillon cube, *or* chicken rice with added chicken bouillon cube, *or* pea with ham, *or* vegetable beef with added beef bouillon cube

Beverage—1 cup Ovaltine *and* 2 cups tea

Jello—⅓ package (lemon, lime, strawberry, raspberry, cherry, orange), *or* pudding, ⅓ package (chocolate, banana, vanilla, butterscotch)

Candy—as above in Lunch

Baked Goods—as above in Breakfast

Fruit—1 cup freeze-dried fruit (strawberries *or* peaches)

Nuts—as above in Lunch

Sugar—½ cup per man on days 1–15 and 26–30, 1 cup per man on
    days 16–25 (1 cup per man proved to be more than we could
    readily use.)
  Salt—1 small shaker for 3-man group per day, plus one large shaker
    in general bag
  Pepper—1 small packet for 3-man group per day
  Butter—as above in Breakfast
  Honey—as above in Breakfast
  Jelly—as above in Breakfast
  Vitamins and Minerals—1 tablet

APPENDIX 6

Suppliers of Specialized Equipment

Alp Sport Inc., Boulder, Colorado—winter expedition tent, anklets, jam tubes

Armour Packing Co. Inc., Chicago, Illinois—freeze-dried meats and vegetables

Eddie Bauer, Seattle, Washington—down clothing, down sleeping bags, shell parkas, socks, net underwear, face mask/stocking caps, stuff sacks, foam pad

Gerry Mountain Sports, Boulder, Colorado—1 liter and ½ liter fuel tins, summit pack, ice ax, shell parka, jam tubes, foam pad, air mattress

Holubar Mountaineering Ltd., Boulder, Colorado—felt boots, ice ax, shell parka

Kelty Pack, Inc., Glendale, California—Kelty BB5 expedition pack-bags and mountaineer frames, frame extensions, dee rings, lashing studs

Mishawaka Rubber Co., Mishawaka, Indiana—Red Ball Oneida insulated rubber boots, closed-cell foam Solar Socks

Recreational Equipment Inc., Seattle, Washington—climbing ropes, stoves, pressure cooker, thermometer, plastic cups, snowshovel, wands, overboots, closed-cell foam pad, air mattress, sling rope, ice screws, carabiners, whistles, pot gripper, first aid manual, Mount McKinley map, fork and spoon sets, aluminum toggles, Swiss Everest goggles, plastic fuel cans, sunburn cream, candle lantern, folding saw, freeze-dried diced ham, freeze-dried strawberries and peaches

Sporthaus Schuster, Munich, Germany—adjustable crampons, leather crampon bindings

U.S. Army Surplus, various outlets in Denver, Colorado—signal mirrors, flare/smoke signals, ski poles, mosquito head nets, arctic shell pants, raw silk gloves, candles